D1117659

The Art of Opinion Writing

Insider Secrets from Top Op-Ed Columnists

By Suzette Martinez Standring

RRP International Publishing LLC
Richmond, Ky. · Greater New Orleans

Copyright©2014, RRP International LLC, DBA Eugenia Ruth LLC,
All rights reserved
No part of this book may be reproduced, stored in a retrieval system
or transmitted by any means without the written permission of the
author or RRP International LLC, DBA Eugenia Ruth LLC

RRP International LLC, DBA Eugenia Ruth LLC
PO Box 1778,
Richmond, Ky. 40476

www.rrpinternational.org

ISBN-13: 978-0-9898848-6-0

Previous Books:

Don McNay's Greatest Hits: Ten Years as an Award-Winning Columnist

Life Lessons from Cancer

Son of a Son of a Gambler: Joe McNay 80ᵗʰ Birthday Edition

Life Lessons from the Golf Course: The Quest for Spiritual Meaning, Psychological Understanding and Inner Peace through the Game of Golf

Life Lessons from the Lottery: Protecting Your Money in a Scary World

Wealth Without Wall Street: A Main Street Guide to Making Money

Son of a Son of a Gambler: Winners, Losers and What to Do When You Win the Lottery

www.rrpinternational.org

Dedication

This is dedicated to all writers who yearn to be read, but worry they lack the skills or a voice important enough to be heard. We all start from this place. This is how you travel forward from here to there.

Table of Contents

Prologue

Opinion writing takes shape from "I support" or "I oppose," and the best op-ed writers can spark a national dialogue, change public policy and bring into the spotlight the invisible and the voiceless.

Being effective carries a price, and not every writer wants to withstand the controversy, hate mail or even death threats that come with the job. Yet those who survive and thrive often transform and enlighten our society. Each columnist in this book boasts career longevity—20 to 40 years—and shares hard-won wisdom about the craft of writing and weathering various battles on the work front.

My initial idea was to feature chapters on the mechanics of op-ed writing as done by some of the best in the business. My assumption was that one's craft expertly applied leads to column writing success. Then I discovered excellent writing is not the whole story.

What each writer brings to the task is unique and therefore vital. Personality, belief, purpose and background create a writing alchemy that affects readers deeply. This became clear interview after interview. Some employ contradictory strategies from each other. Many pioneer new areas. Every columnist sets out on an individual journey to learn how to convey the personal pronoun "I" with fearlessness and effect, and arriving at that destination takes place in different ways.

Perhaps just like you, the columnists in this book had a difficult if not downright unlikely trek to the summit, fighting the odds, often with no guidance, slogging forward with little or no support at the start of their careers. Perhaps just like you, they were driven to stand out in a very competitive field.

This is the rare writing guidebook that brings together inspiration, encouragement, and technique. Each chapter features an op-ed columnist who shares his/her personal struggles and triumphs, as well as practical advice about opinion writing.

Career longevity is to be prized, and writing about change does change one personally in the process. Most of the featured op-ed columnists are Pulitzer Prize winners and finalists, and recipients of journalism's highest awards. Official recognition only echoes what everyday readers know from following such a writer's work, and that is, "This columnist makes a difference."

If you're reading this book, it may be you can make a difference, too.

Suzette Martinez Standring, Author
June 2013

"Few will have the greatness to bend history itself; but each of us can work to change a small portion of events, and in the total of all those acts will be written the history of this generation."
-Robert F. Kennedy (1925-1968)

DAVE ASTOR

Op-ed Columnists, Then and Now

It may seem odd to feature a reporter's view at the beginning of a book about opinion columnists, but the newspaper industry is changing as fast and frequently as Kim Kardashian's outfits. A lay of the land is in order. For aspiring op-ed writers, a look at the rear view mirror is helpful if only to realize the size of shoes to be filled. Even the most seasoned columnists wonder about the direction of professional public opinion given the explosion of blogs and commentators. Dave Astor, a veteran reporter since 1983, weighs in with the "then and now" of op-ed writing.

Astor's eye-opening memoir in 2012 charts an almost 30-year history of covering columnists and cartoonists in *Comic (and Column) Confessional: Finding Myself While Covering Syndicates, Celebrities, and a Changing Media World*, written as the former senior editor and syndication reporter for *Editor and Publisher Magazine*.

There's bad news and good news on how the evolution of the newspaper industry affects today's opinion writers.

First, the days of the All Powerful Op-Ed Oz are over. Opinion columnists do not wield the influence and power they once had. Astor said, "In the past, columnists such as Walter Lippmann, James Reston of *The New York Times* and Jack Anderson had a bigger impact because of the huge number of newspapers that carried them. Back then they were the only game in town. Presidents listened to them."

Now it's a different game. Competing with Internet news and independent blogs, print newspaper circulation and syndication numbers are down. For example, almost 1,000 newspapers carried columnist Jack Anderson in his heyday. In comparison, George Will is a top syndicated columnist at 368 total papers, according to a national study by mediamatters.org. Another source Tribune Media Services deems Cal Thomas the most widely syndicated political columnist with over 500 newspapers. Whatever way syndication success is determined, the numbers are still far below rates from yesteryear.

Today the no-holds-barred, political muckraking style of Jack Anderson that sold papers in the 1950s and 60s would give pause to modern editors. Astor noted, "Newspapers might not want to antagonize what readers they might still have."

Also, times have changed in favor of diversity. Astor said, "Back in the 1930s through 1950s, it was virtually all white men, with the occasional exception, but nowadays there are more women, more people of color and that's a good thing."

And with a diversity of writers, the style of opinion writing has evolved dramatically. Modern columnists draw from their backgrounds and personal interests to speak to larger issues and to create a special identity in the field of op-ed.

What happens in society is viewed in ways unique to the opinion writer, according to Astor, the vice president (2012-2013) of the National Society of Newspaper Columnists, "Nowadays there are different ways of describing an op-ed column. You can take your personal life and make it universal, using it as a springboard to talk about politics or social issues."

For example, Connie Schultz, a former columnist for the *Cleveland Plain Dealer*, shared personal stories to resonate with readers about big picture realities, as when she wrote about her working class father. Another piece spotlighted how management pocketed money in a tip jar, an injustice to employees, and it proved to be a column that helped Schultz to win the 2005 Pulitzer Prize for Distinguished Commentary.

Joanna Weiss of *The Boston Globe* served as an entertainment critic before writing opinion. Her forte is observing how pop culture is reflected in politics. Lynne Varner of *The Seattle Times* began her career as a journalist reporting on the city's school system. Varner believes many of society's ills can be traced to a failure in education, which she now seeks to address as an op-ed writer.

Astor said, "Those who give op-ed a personal touch would have been very unusual long ago."

Making a name for one's self in this field is no longer limited to newspaper employees. Today's 24-7 news cycle, in traditional media and online, has an unlimited appetite for commentary. It opens the door to anyone determined to feed the beast. What will separate a winner from the wannabe will be credibility, accuracy and stellar writing. Astor warns the novice to tread carefully at first.

Generally, op-ed writing is not best accomplished right after college. Aspiring journalists should realize that opinion writing requires significant life experience because maturity leads to insights that resonate with readers. That is not to say that a young adult is not capable of a meaningful opinion. However, a writer earns credibility over the course of time and hard-won experience.

Many op-ed columnists began as reporters and were trained to follow leads, uncover the facts, report with accuracy and write under deadline. Such skills form a strong foundation for column writing. Paying one's dues includes developing a solid reporting background.

Astor himself followed a pattern of reporter-to-columnist. Since 2003, he has written a humorous op-ed column for *The Montclair Times* in New Jersey. Astor conveys his opinions with a quirky twist. His advice column uses a mock question and answer format as a setup for satire on local and current issues. In 2013 the New Jersey Press Association awarded *The Montclair Times*, "Best Editorial

Section," of which Astor shared.

"I guess I like to do word play and the Q&A format gives me an opportunity to do that, especially in the signatures of the fake questioners. Subliminally, after reading and covering advice columnists for so many years on my day job—Heloise, Abby and Ann Landers—I found that format comfortable to write. And I thought it would be an opportunity to use humor, I've always liked to write humor, getting people to laugh while making a strong point at the same time. I think it goes down easier because readers are being entertained and not being beaten over the head with a point," Astor said.

The veteran journalist reveals what has worked best for longevity and success in this ever-changing industry.

Dave Astor's Writing Process, Insights and Advice

Filling the tool belt. Astor has been a journalist for more than 30 years, with 10 years as an op-ed columnist, and believes the following skills and tools are important:

Create a body of sources and key contacts.

Have a familiarity with how systems work (town, county, state, federal, corporate).

Establish one's identity and credibility as a journalist with memorable, accurate writing.

Have an ability to gain trust and to relate to others.

Achieve strong writing skills from writing regularly under deadline.

Astor now writes as a freelancer, and is mindful of using his reputation to land writing assignments elsewhere. For example, he blogs about books for *The Huffington Post* to expand professional exposure and he offers this advice:

Create a blog with a significant following.

Meet colleagues, editors and other key people at professional meetings and conferences. Use those contacts for opportunities to submit freelance pieces to newspapers or online publications.

Write a book to create an identity as a subject expert.

Offer new information gained from good reporting and source development.

Create a reputation for well-reasoned opinions, solid facts and a memorable writing style.

Consider submitting pieces for free, for a limited time, to get your foot in a publication's door.

Astor remains upbeat. "Nothing is impossible, especially with your own blog. Being a current or former reporter can give you more credibility, but now if you just have knowledge and a lively writing voice, you could probably still pull off an op-ed type of column, especially if you're doing it online."

Montclairvoyant: In 2016, will Manhattan be a suburb of high-density Montclair?

By Dave Astor
April 18, 2013
The Montclair (NJ) Times

During a brief trip to the future in a (very) Smart car, I saw this "Montclairvoyant" column from April 2016. It seems like the plan to "Manhattanize" our town succeeded beyond the wildest dreams of Robert Jackson, MD (Mayor/Developer).

DEAR MONTCLAIRVOYANT,
Here in 2016, Montclair has so many tall buildings blocking my eastward view that I can no longer see New York City! Or Ed Koch!
Sincerely,
Viewless and Clueless
Um…is that because he died in 2013?

DEAR MONTCLAIRVOYANT,
With the 102-story CentroVertical building in the way, I also can't see the Empire State Building!
Sincerely,
Don Draper-Skyscraper
Ask a Montclair artist to paint a picture of that building on CentroVertical's western wall. If you pay fairly, she might add King Kong.

DEAR MONTCLAIRVOYANT,
The high-density development near train stations was supposed to mean less use of cars and more use of mass transit. But residents of a suburb like Montclair still need to drive to places such as church.
Sincerely,
Dashboard of Trustees
When churchgoers drive to mass, that's mass transit.

DEAR MONTCLAIRVOYANT,
Hell awaits you, Wordplay Guy. With eight million new residents and cars, how bad has Montclair's traffic become here in 2016?
Sincerely,
Gridlock Ness Monster
My kid got on the school bus this morning, and arrived at school just in time to board the bus home.

DEAR MONTCLAIRVOYANT,
Speaking of schools, Montclair had to build 11 more since 2013 to handle the children of new residents, and the new debt costs more to pay down than the new ratables coming in.
Sincerely,
The Sum of All Fears
Meanwhile, the faux Italian and faux Spanish names of those schools are getting on my nerves. Elbow Macaroni High?

DEAR MONTCLAIRVOYANT,
How bad is the 2016 parking situation?
Sincerely,
Spaces I Remember
I drove to the Wellmont to see a British band, and the closest space I could find was in England.

DEAR MONTCLAIRVOYANT,
The Moody Blues?
Sincerely,
Hayward Just In
Yes, BlueWaveNJ members are among the residents morose about the urbanization of Montclair.

Montclairvoyant: A town full of eateries features lots of catering (to developers)

By Dave Astor
April 27, 2013
The Montclair (NJ) Times

DEAR MONTCLAIRVOYANT,
Montclairites and millions of others have worked so hard for
sensible gun control, yet Congress remains cowed by the NRA.
Comment?
Sincerely,
How Now, Kowtow
My favorite mythical things are Bigfoot and politicians with
backbones.

DEAR MONTCLAIRVOYANT,
Do gun manufacturers care about anything other than profits?
Sincerely,
Blood Money Men
How dare you impugn the motives of those patriotic companies!
They care about something much more important than profits—
freedom (to make MORE profits).

DEAR MONTCLAIRVOYANT,
Speaking of the rich getting richer, developers love the high-density
projects that will soon mar Montclair. How can they ever thank
Robert Jackson, MD (Mayor/Developer), for going against the
wishes of most voters?
Sincerely,
Master Plan: Disaster Plan
Those developers (who basically run Montclair) can thank the mayor
by renaming our tall-skyline town Jackson Heights.

DEAR MONTCLAIRVOYANT,
Queens?
Sincerely,

Edgar Rice Borough
Greedy developers do think they're royalty, but most are men.

DEAR MONTCLAIRVOYANT,
Will you keep putting "MD" after Robert Jackson's name in future weeks?
Sincerely,
Dee Ductible
(Removes stethoscope from ears.) Please return to this column's waiting room while I check the heartbeat of a politician who favors the onerous NRA over gun victims. Oops—no heart.

DEAR MONTCLAIRVOYANT,
Montclair's Planning Board, which has approved various overdevelopment schemes in recent years, has a big say in the new Master Plan. Isn't that like a fox guarding the hen house?
Sincerely,
Open Space? Erase!
Board members approved so many variances for that hen house that it's now bigger than the "Stone Eagles" mansion. Call it..."Stone Hens."

DEAR MONTCLAIRVOYANT,
Robert Jackson, MD, says developers will pay for at least some infrastructure improvements as Montclair becomes citified. Will developers also fund new public schools for the children of new residents?
Sincerely,
The Desk Set
No. But those landowning moguls will be glad to fully endow a chair—a metal folding one.

DEAR MONTCLAIRVOYANT,
The upcoming Montclair Film Festival sounds terrific, but $100-$125 for the opening gala? That's economic segregation in a liberal town with many residents who can't afford high-priced tickets.
Sincerely,
Cinema and Pa

Perhaps the less-affluent can sell printouts of the new Master Plan on eBay. That should fund a few nanoseconds at the MFF party.

"Anaxagoras said to a man who was grieving because he was dying in a foreign land, 'The descent to Hades is the same from every place.'"
- Diogenes Laertius (early 3rd century)

JOEL BRINKLEY

Foreign Affairs as Op-Ed

Joel Brinkley grew up with politics, international affairs and current issues. The famed newscaster, David M. Brinkley, is his dad. Today Joel Brinkley belongs to a rare breed: the foreign affairs op-ed columnist. "I think there are only four or five of us in the U.S. I've traveled all over the world, and I've been to over 50 countries. Foreign affairs fascinate me and I've developed a strong expertise in this area."

In 1980, Brinkley was awarded the Pulitzer Prize for International Reporting regarding his coverage of the Khmer Rouge regime in Cambodia. He served for 23 years as foreign correspondent for the *New York Times*. Brinkley now lives in California where he teaches journalism at Stanford University and is syndicated with Tribune Media Services for his foreign affairs op-ed column. Featured on TMS' *American Voices,* Brinkley offers a global perspective as a member of a team that includes columnists Robert Reich, Rachel Marsden and Ta-Nehisi Coates.

When asked why he chose journalism as a career, Brinkley said, "I just love to write. That's who I am, and I've been a writer since I graduated from college." His career with *The New York Times* began as a reporter and he traveled worldwide to break news on bombings, drug cartels, wars and disasters.

Seeing events unfold through fresh eyes set his reporting apart. According to Brinkley, reporters based in a region for a long time can develop jaded perspectives. They feel they know so much about a subject that it no longer bears reporting. It was one of the reasons *The New York Times* sent new reporters to such areas, as when Brinkley was assigned to Cambodia in 1979.

"I immersed myself in refugee camps in Cambodia in ways that no one else did. I had never been to Southeast Asia, and so I saw things that some foreign correspondents didn't see any longer," he said.

In 2006, Brinkley needed a change from reporting. Six months after leaving his post with *The New York Times,* he turned to opinion writing. "I want readers to understand important parts of the world in ways they might not otherwise."

For his syndicated column of 750 words, Brinkley writes about news in other countries that may not be covered widely elsewhere, and he said, "For example, I filed a column about politics in Egypt to destroy the pyramids because they are symbols of idolatry. I follow events around the world. I have several ideas and I pick one."

A longtime background in news analysis and research serve him well. However, in the beginning as an op-ed columnist, he had difficulty writing in the first person. He had not offered personal commentary in his previous job as a daily journalist, and so it took a while before he could. "I still had the practice of coming to a conclusion, and calling someone else to say it. Having the confidence to draw assumptions from the facts on my own without relying on other people to do that was the hardest thing for me in transitioning from news writing to opinion writing."

Those sharing Brinkley's passion for foreign affairs should seek opportunities to follow international stories. Many reporters cover U.S. government and its various branches of operations that are intertwined with foreign governments, such as Afghanistan, Iraq and China. A reporter could ask to pursue a story in China, for example, and land a residential foreign assignment.

"You can't start writing a foreign affairs column unless you've been a foreign correspondent, or served abroad. These days it is a lot harder to be a foreign correspondent, but so much of what happens in American government is related to foreign issues," he said.

Brinkley landed a syndicated spot as an op-ed columnist after he left *The New York Times* to teach at Stanford University in California. "The way I did it, I put on a conference in Stanford the first year I was here. I met the editor of the *San Francisco Chronicle*, and I asked to write a foreign affairs column in May 2007. In fall 2007, I approached McClatchy-Tribune News Service to distribute the column. In the summer of 2010, Creators Syndicate approached me, but frankly what they offered to pay was not sufficient. So I approached Tribune Media Services and sent them some of my columns. We've been going on together ever since."

Joel Brinkley's Writing Process, Insights, and Advice

A columnist must be entrepreneurial. "Being a column writer doesn't come to you. You have to be entrepreneurial. You have to be aggressive and have a background that will convince people you are the right person to write that column."

Have lots of ideas. "Idea generation is the ability to look at an event and come up with unique ways to write about it. That trait may be learned or innate, but many journalists have to generate ideas. I usually come up with four or five and pick one."

Have one theme per column. Hit one important idea and support it in a variety of ways within 750 words.

Write for the simplest member of your audience. Assume some readers know little about anything in your column. That is safest. Don't lard columns with jargon or issues you cannot explain.

Inform. There is no time when information is too much. "I always over-report. I don't think it's possible to inundate a reader in 750 words."

Research. "I always do far more research than I have the space to use it. It gives me the confidence to write what is well-informed."

Getting sources to talk: According to Brinkley, encouraging reluctant sources to talk is harder for a columnist compared to a reporter because a column may not be as widely read as a news story. Therefore, the threat of "I'll just write that you refused to talk to me," may not be effective.

Brinkley added, "However, every story has two sides. If I want somebody on one side to talk to me, I tell them that the other party has spoken to me, and I don't think they should be allowed to say [fill in the blank.]"

For his readers, Joel Brinkley opens a window to the workings of world governments. It requires a keen eye and steady grasp on the essential question of what is going on and why. A full immersion background similar to his may be difficult to acquire, but for the like-minded, foreign affairs op-ed offers an exciting, global platform.

National leaders go abroad when they get sick

By Joel Brinkley
August 28, 2012
Tribune Media Services

Meles Zenawi, Ethiopia's dictator, died last week—in a Brussels hospital.

Why didn't he get medical care at home? Look at the state of his people's health, and you'll understand.

The government provides vaccinations for only 5 percent of the children. Fewer still receive antibiotics when they contract pneumonia. Only 20 percent of teenage girls are educated about AIDS. Is it any wonder that Ethiopia's average life expectancy is 56—among the world's lowest?

Eleven years ago, 53 African nations signed a pledge to spend at least 15 percent of their national budgets on health care. Almost no nation has lived up to that. Right now, Ethiopia dedicates 3.6 percent of its budget to health. So no one was surprised when the president went abroad for care.

In fact, across the developing world whenever a president or potentate gets sick, he travels to a more developed state for care. That boldly displays the heedless view these leaders have of their own people. Perhaps if they were required to use their own hospitals, they might be more inclined to improve them.

Many of these reprobates find they can't step on the plane as blithely as Zenawi did. To get away often requires stealth and deceit.

Not long ago, Asif Ali Zardari, Pakistan's president, wanted to go abroad for an unspecified, apparently minor health issue. So he directed doctors at a Karachi hospital to forge a report saying he had a more significant illness: prostate cancer. Dr. Ghayur Ayub, a former national director general of health, had a look at the lab results and on his blog declared the diagnosis "ludicrous." Zardari left anyway.

Last year, he decided to spend some time in Dubai. His spokesmen said he'd gone to visit his children. But that was proved to be a lie after he entered a hospital. The rambunctious Pakistan press declared that he was being treated for a host of different problems: a heart attack, a clot in his neck, a dangerous reaction to medicine.

After he'd been away two weeks, the news media began writing about the political message Zardari was sending. Pulse International, Pakistan's most prominent medical journal, wrote that Zardari's trip demonstrated a "lack of trust and confidence in Pakistani healthcare professionals and healthcare institutions." (It turned out he'd had a minor stroke.)

Zardari is hardly alone. Since Hugo Chavez, the Venezuelan strongman, took office in 1999, he has bragged ceaselessly about improving health care for his people. But when he contracted cancer, he flew off to Cuba—twice. That's a telling statement about Venezuelan medicine. Cuban doctors say they earn about $24 a month.

In Venezuela, rumors are rife that Chavez's cancer is fatal, though he denies that. Is he lying? You decide. Chavez suddenly decided to build a $140-million mausoleum for Simon Bolivar, the 19th century political and military leader Chavez reveres. The Venezuelan press notes that the building has room for at least one more resident.

Hun Sen, Cambodia's prime minister, visited constituents a while back and noted that he had a minor wound needing treatment. He insisted that only when "doctors in Cambodia say they cannot deal with it will I go to a hospital abroad." He failed to note that a few years earlier he had traveled to Tokyo for what the government said was a two-day "checkup." Cambodian doctors aren't capable of even that? Like the other leaders who travel abroad, health and welfare conditions in his country are no better than those in Ethiopia.

But in Saudi Arabia, an exceedingly wealthy state, Crown Prince Nayef said he was traveling abroad for "medical tests" this spring. He was gone a month and said he'd been in a Cleveland hospital but provided no other details. He died in June—in a Geneva hospital.

Dictators always seem to be traveling abroad for simple tests or checkups. Nursultan Nazarbayev, Kazakhstan's president, insisted he was in a German hospital for a "checkup" last year—though he had issued a press release saying, "I suggest everyone have routine checkups here in Kazakhstan." A German paper reported that he was treated for prostate cancer.

This spring, a South African newspaper reported that government leaders from Malawi, Gabon, Togo, Nigeria and Tanzania all had died in foreign hospitals. The paper then made a note of a fact that every one of those leaders' constituents ought to stand up and shout about: These heads of state "prefer to pour taxpayer's money into overseas medical facilities rather than spending it on improving health care at home."

China a long way from gaining world's trust

By Joel Brinkley
April 2, 2013
Tribune Media Services

On his first foreign foray as China's new president, Xi Jinping
visited Russia and then Tanzania, two countries with which China
has frosty relations at best.

"China and Russia, as the biggest neighbors of each other, share
many commonalities," Xi declared in Moscow. But in truth the two
nations carry on carefully crafted civility, and that's all.

"All of Africa is China's friend," Xi said in Dar es Salaam, Tazania.
But many Africans say they hold a different view.

"China takes our primary goods and sells us manufactured ones,"
Lamido Sanusi, Nigeria's central-bank governor, wrote in the
Financial Times last month. This, he scoffed, is "the essence of
colonialism."

China is earnestly striving to become a respected world power, one
that finally surpasses the United States. The day could conceivably
come when its economy, even its military, are larger than America's.
But its biggest problem right now, one that's much harder to correct,
is the nation's "soft power." China appears to have very few true
friends in the world.

Its belligerent, assertive stance on territorial rights in the South
China Sea the last few years has driven away almost every Asian
nation. Nearly all of them are now asking the U.S. for help—even
Vietnam. China's only regional "friend" is Cambodia, a nation
Beijing has virtually purchased with $8 billion in aid over the last
few years and another $5 billion promised. Hun Sen, Cambodia's
prime minister, no longer openly disparages China.

Beijing used to count Burma as its friend, but Burma's ongoing transition toward democracy came about in large part because Burma's rulers didn't like being dependent on Beijing. North Korea and China routinely criticize each other, but for political reasons they remain inseparable.

China experts point to other allies: Zimbabwe, Iran, Cuba, Sudan—all brutal authoritarian states like China. Venezuela was an ally under Hugo Chavez, but now that he's dead, the future relationship is unknown. Syria was also friendly, but its future is even less clear.

China is sucking up to Pakistan as America's relationship with that country continues to sour. But Pakistan is likely to go with whomever can offer the most lucrative aid packages. As Husain Haqqani, former Pakistani ambassador to the U.S., told me, "China will give them rifles, but they can't give F-16 aircraft."

Beijing solicits an alliance with Serbia, siding with it in the ongoing debate about Kosovo's independence—even though just last week a war-crimes tribunal convicted two senior Bosnian Serbs of directing a campaign of murder, torture and persecution during the Bosnian war 20 years ago.

What about the rest of the world? Why does China have so few friends? Put simply, China faces trust issues all over the world.

Would you trust a government that tells its people: No worries: the water is clean—after more than 16,000 diseased, decomposing pigs were found in the river that supplies water for Shanghai's 23 million people? One resident told the *London Telegraph*, "I'm worried about the drinking water. It really, really stinks."

How about a nation whose students routinely cheat on applications to foreign colleges and universities, according to a report by a college consulting firm there? "Cheating is pervasive in China, driven by hyper-competitive parents and aggressive agents," Zinch China reported. "Our research indicated that 90 percent of recommendation letters are fake, 70 percent of essays are not written by the applicant and 50 percent of high-school transcripts are falsified."

How trustworthy would you find a nation whose young men come to America, infiltrate the workforce, steal industrial secrets and then take them home? Last week, a federal court sentenced Chinese citizen Sixing Liu to nearly six years in prison for passing thousands of files from a military contractor to Beijing.

Sixing's conviction was the latest of about 100 similar cases involving Chinese infiltrators in the past four years.

Not every problem is so grand. Late last month, according to multiple sources, the Swedish car maker Volvo complained that some of its Chinese dealerships had inflated sales figures to qualify for cash bonuses—when in fact Volvo sales had actually declined.

By now you see the pattern.

Even a senior Chinese official acknowledged that the government often fakes its national economic statistics, like the GDP, inflation and unemployment rates. He once called them "man-made," according to a leaked U.S. diplomatic cable.

Speaking at a university in Moscow last month, President Xi acknowledged that "no country or bloc of countries can again single-handedly dominate world affairs." His unspoken target: the United States and Europe.

But given China's frequent dishonest behavior, that nation won't soon dominate world affairs, either.

"You can teach someone who cares to write columns, but you can't teach someone who writes columns to care."
- Ellen Goodman

ELLEN GOODMAN

The Personal is Political

In the 1960s a woman's opinion was rare on a newspaper's op-ed page. Instead female interests, as deemed by the industry, were relegated and limited to the food and fashion sections.

Ellen Goodman remembers, early in her career, working for *Newsweek Magazine* when women did research and men wrote the articles. In the 1960s the Women's Movement battled gender inequality on all fronts, and feminism directly led to Goodman's career as a *Boston Globe* opinion columnist in 1974. "I wanted to take down the wall between the personal and the political, between the women's pages and the op-ed pages. I thought they were artificial distinctions because that's not the way we live."

The Feminist Movement galvanized the national mindset against the imposition of unfair politics and presumption at home and at work. As a result, a fast-changing culture affected the way women lived, including Goodman. "It was the largest social change of my lifetime, and not that many women were writing about it in newspapers. It was a huge new grid to put over our lives and over our world."

Goodman was one of the first op-ed columnists to show how the highly personal is very political. First as a reporter in 1964, and then a columnist in 1974 (syndicated with The Washington Post Writers Group since 1976), and through her retirement in 2010, she remains an author, public speaker and one of the nation's leading syndicated columnists. Throughout her career Goodman has been lauded with journalism's highest awards, including the 1980 Pulitzer Prize for Distinguished Commentary and the Ernie Pyle Lifetime Achievement Award from the National Society of Newspaper

Columnists in 2008.

She is iconic for chronicling social change and women's issues, but she views her life's work in a much broader sense. "If I had to put a subject over the column that I wrote over the years, the subject would be values."

Few can boast Goodman's column's longevity or her ranking among the top five columnists in the country. "Part of the reason that it lasted a long time was that even when people disagreed with me, they were interested in following my train of thought and believed that I had something worth listening to."

In describing the essence of good reporting and how it factored into her success, Goodman said, "I'm a pretty good listener and I have a pretty good sense of what is going on around me. That's the reporting piece. Reporting meaning being a person in the world who pays attention. People often say to me, 'You wrote just what I was thinking.' I didn't write what they were thinking. I wrote what they were thinking about. My job was to figure out what it meant.

"So I think I helped people figure out the issues that were confusing or troubling because I had my ear to the ground. For women I think I affirmed a lot of the experiences they were having, and the Women's Movement was about discovering they were not the only ones."

Goodman's work exemplifies respect for her readers—supporters and detractors alike—but she wondered if civility is a fading virtue. "I have always believed that people appreciate, understand, and accept new ideas and that you should be respectful to those who disagree with you. That may be a very unique point of view right now when there is a lot of food fight journalism," Goodman said.

Today, many columnists and commentators promote a take-no-prisoners attitude instead of advocating a strong, intelligent position on an issue. Too often shocking sound bites trump a clear viewpoint. "If you write from a narrow, pretty didactic point of view, you may get a lot of attention—it's like screaming in a public place—but you probably won't last a long time. You won't really have an effect. You'll only have an effect on the people who already agree with you.

"My goal was to have people say, "Hah! I didn't think about it that way."

Goodman confided her little secret for avoiding TV show appearances, "I tell them I have mixed feelings." She explained that shows prefer black and white positions, combative points and counterpoints. She is a fighter who knows that life is complicated.

In Goodman's writing, research is key to creativity and credibility. It's not just about gathering data to bolster an argument. She uses investigation to address novel questions, explore fresh approaches and suggest new directions. "I've been a classic over-reporter all my life. A lot of it ended up on the cutting room floor, but a lot of it ended up, too, as part of my thought process, part of thinking something out."

When crafting an opinion column, Goodman proceeds with thoroughness and the time required. Other journalistic demands—blogging posts, emails and tweets—can shortchange thoughtful assessment, which is so vital to powerful, well-written commentary.

All deadlines are not equal, according to Goodman. "I made my living telling people what I think, but you have to have time to think. Everything has gotten faster and shorter and more demanding. The only thing that hasn't changed is the amount of time it takes to think something through. So, when we tell people to keep posting and tweeting, then what is the sum total of what those posts and tweets are?

"You have to make some decisions about what matters to you, and I understand that can be hard under the gun. But again, do you want to have an effect? Do you actually want to help people understand something? I've always thought that column writing is in the business of making sense, and you can't make sense of the world in

140 characters." Blogs, social media, and online news are booming even as newspaper readership is declining. The number of bloggers rises, but the bloggers' challenge is to reach outside their fan base. Goodman said, "Let's face it, newspapers don't have the power or reach they once did, so newspaper columnists no longer have the power or the reach they once did. Bloggers can have a lot of power.

"But one of the problems of blogging is that, by and large, they are blogging to the converted. The world has changed so much that people are much more fragmented. Newspapers go across demographics and political beliefs, but you have to like bloggers, literally in the Facebook sense of the word, to listen to them. They are much more of a closed circle.

"There are a million blogs in the naked city, and some of them are thoughtful and interesting, some of them are funny and snarky, some of them are a complete, total waste of time. I think while bloggers will become widely read and known, it's harder."

Ellen Goodman's Writing Process, Insights, and Advice

Goodman is an early morning person. She gets on her treadmill or takes a walk. "I find movement helps your brain." She likes to complete research for a column the day before she writes it. On deadline day, her writing begins in the morning at home. "In my mind, I try to sketch out in a very loose way, a first draft. Then I write in a quick and dirty, not much more than bullet points, kind of way. Then I go to the office and sit down and get a first draft done before lunch. I have always been a classic rewrite person, so I rewrite until I have to hit the send button." She added that the time it takes to write her column varies from three hours to "forever."

Write what you believe. Op-ed writers do follow topical news, but Goodman pointed out, "Opinion writers should follow what really interests them and then learn about it. Over time you probably are attracted to some of the same issues and you will write about them again and again, but often in a newer and deeper way. I don't think you could possibly know about Afghanistan on Monday, Syria on Tuesday and Sri Lanka on Wednesday. You just can't. On the other hand, you can understand something about say, bio-ethics. When another case comes up, you research it and it's deeper and it has a different spin on it, and then you go into that. As things in the news change, you are efficient when you continually learn something new."

A column's goal: The size of a column is time enough to make an argument.

Key components in opinion writing: "You need a beginning, a middle and an end. Every column is a story in that you need to give people the facts, as you understand them, and an understanding of the issue. Sometimes it's a personal story, and you hope it has a through-line that leads to a conclusion with a kicker of some kind, an ending that satisfies as you're leaving it. I'd say beginnings and endings are very important. If the editor cuts the ending off, it's really not a happy day."

Writing voice: "After a while you get the rhythm of your own voice in your mind. I'll say one thing. I always wrote in my own voice, and very often people say, 'Where did you find your voice?' as if it's a lucky penny on the street. You don't find your voice. You release your voice. So for me, over time, it became easier to write the way I sound. It became more and more a part of who I was."

Taking a stand on complex issues. What does Goodman use as her compass when deciding where to land on complicated matter? "It's usually reporting. The more you learn, the more it fits into whatever perspective you have on life and what you think is right."

Retirement opens bigger doors. Goodman retired in 2010 from op-ed writing, the same year she co-founded with Len Fishman The Conversation Project (www.conversationproject.org), how to honor end-of-life wishes for loved ones, especially if such people are no longer able to voice or make their own decisions at that critical time. It began with a circle of concerned colleagues, and now it has become a national movement to get families talking before it's too late.

Goodman said, "The Conversation Project is a public engagement campaign to get everyone's end of life wishes expressed and respected. We know that everyone has a story of a 'good death' or a 'hard death,' and we know that the difference between those two stories is often whether they have the conversation.

"In the year before my mother's death I was faced with a lot of decisions for which I was unprepared and blindsided and I began to realize that this was a very common experience. How much easier could this have been if we had had a real conversation about what our loved one wanted at the end of their life. The Conversation Project is a place to start."

For almost 40 years, Ellen Goodman has put the female perspective foremost on national op-ed pages, and even in retirement, she continues. Goodman said, "We are generally people who worry about our weight and nuclear holocaust, and it seemed to me that some of the biggest public policy issues of our times are also related to our personal lives."

She's Ready to Play

By Ellen Goodman
July 16, 2009
Washington Post Writers Group

I have long been a collector of sports metaphors, but I never expected such a treasure of memorabilia to come out of a Senate hearing room. At times it sounded more like the all-star game than the confirmation of a Supreme Court justice. I could have organized an office pool guessing the number of times senators would say "balls and strikes" (13) or "umpire" (16).

The members of the Judiciary Committee riffed on the idea of judge-as-umpire.

Alas, no comment could trump Alabama Sen. Jeff Sessions' pre-hearing pitch for a "blindfolded justice calling the balls and strikes fairly and objectively."

YES! Just what we need in the big leagues! An umpire wearing a blindfold!

But this was not just jock-talk. Or a play for impartiality. It was a thinly veiled anxiety attack at the idea that Sonia Sotomayor might be a team player for Liberals vs. Conservatives or, worse yet, the Girls and Latina Team vs. the White Boys. The specter haunting Sotomayor was that "Wise Latina Woman."

What seemed radical to the Republican committeemen was her hint that a WLW "with the richness of her experiences" might make wiser decisions than ... THEM! She might even, as Texas Sen. John Cornyn said darkly, want to "advance causes or groups."

This was the lineup at the hearings. Sotomayor sat stoically while a pugnacious Sessions lectured her on the role of a judge and a patronizing Lindsey Graham told her she had a reputation as a "bit of a bully."

The would-be first Latina justice faced a committee with only two women members in order to get confirmed by a Senate with only 17 women for a seat on a court with only one other woman. And yet Sotomayor had to prove that *she* wasn't biased: "Men and women [are] equally capable of being wise and fair judges."

Also at stake—or at bat if you prefer—were the judge's earlier musings about the importance of different life experiences: "I simply do not know exactly what that difference will be in my judging. But I accept there will be some based on gender and my Latina heritage."

She also said: "I wonder whether by ignoring our differences as women or men of color we do a disservice both to the law and society." A horrified Sessions called this "philosophically incompatible with the American system."

I am, of course, charmed to see conservatives decrying gender differences as un-American since they long used differences to justify women's second-class status. Better they should turn their wrath on talk show host G. Gordon Liddy, who said of Sotomayor: "Let's hope that the key conferences aren't when she's menstruating."

It was women who fought the idea that men and women were intrinsically different and therefore unequal. But by the time Sotomayor became a judge, more women felt free to "wonder": Did we have to fit the (male) norm to be equal, or could we change it?

Wasn't it OK—even important—for women to bring a different perspective to the table when talking about science, violence, business? Couldn't they bring a different perspective to the bench when listening to Lilly Ledbetter plead for equal pay, or to a 13-year-old who was strip-searched?

A wise Latina woman doesn't engage in a philosophical discussion while the boys are talking sports. But in my experience, when women are asked to "rise above" their experience, to ignore the difference in background, they are often being told to expunge the female and to think/work/live/rule like a man.

Score one for the status quo.

Clarence Thomas, a fierce advocate for impartiality, has said with icy passion, "In order to be a judge, a person must attempt to exorcise himself or herself of the passions, thoughts, and emotions that fill any frail human being. He must become almost pure, in the way that fire purifies metal, before he can decide a case."

Compare that to Sotomayor's comment Tuesday that we are not robots: "I think the system is strengthened when judges don't assume they're impartial."

Yes, we are more than a sum total of our experiences. No, the huge majority of cases have nothing to do with race or gender, or being a diabetic for that matter. Yes, judges see through their own lens and beyond it.

But if I may revert to the sports metaphor, this judge who thinks deeply about both life and the law is ready to take the field for the Supremes.

Looking backward, looking forward

By Ellen Goodman
January 1, 2010
The Boston Globe

(Editor's note: This is Ellen Goodman's final column. She has graced these pages with insight and inspiration for decades. We wish her a joyous and fulfilling retirement.)

There is something fitting about writing my last column on the first day of a new year. January, after all, is named for the Roman god of beginnings and endings. He looked backward and forward at the same time. So, this morning, do I.

I wish I could find the right language to describe this rite of passage. Retirement, that swoon of a word, just won't do. The Spanish translation, *jubilacion*, is a bit over the top for my own mix of feelings.

The phrase that kept running through my head as I considered this next step was: "I'm letting myself go." Yes, I can imagine the response if a tweet came across the screen announcing, "Ellen Goodman has let herself go." I can see the illustration: out of shape, lazy, slovenly, the very worst things you can whisper about a woman of a certain age.

But I love the idea of reclaiming that phrase. After all, where will you go when you let yourself go? To let this question fill the free space between deadlines in my life has been quite liberating. It suggests the freedom that can fuel this journey.

Looking backward and forward. I belong to a generation that has transformed our culture. We've been the change agents for civil rights, women's rights, gay rights.

Now, we find ourselves on the cutting edge of another huge social change. This time, it's the longevity revolution. Ours is the first generation to collectively cross the demarcation line of senior citizenship with actuarial tables on our side.

"Senior citizen" is now a single demographic name tag that includes those who fought in World War II and those who were born in World War II. We don't have a label yet to describe the early, active aging. But many of us are pausing to recalculate the purpose of a longer life. We are reinventing ourselves and society's expectations, just as we have throughout our lives.

Looking backward and forward. I began writing my column when my daughter was seven and I leave as my grandson turns seven. I began writing about Gerald Ford and end writing about Barack Obama. I began on a typewriter, transmitting columns on a Xerox telecopier. Now I have a MacBook on my desk and an iPhone in my pocket.

I celebrated my lucky midlife marriage in these pages, sent my daughter to college, welcomed my grandchildren, said farewell to my mother. I upheld Thanksgiving traditions in this space and celebrated them with a family that evolved far beyond my grandparents' idea of tradition. I wrote about values and pushed back against those who believe they own the patent on this word.

It has been a great gift to make a living trying to make sense out of the world around me. That is as much a disposition as an occupation.

Now, when people ask what are you going to do next, I am tempted to co-opt Susan Stamberg's one-word answer when she left her anchor post at NPR: "Less." I am more tempted to say, simply, "We'll see." After 46 years of deadlines, it is time to take in some oxygen, to breathe and consider.

At the risk of sounding like a politician one step ahead of the sheriff, I want to spend more time with my family and fulfill the fantasy of a summer on my porch in Maine. But of course writers write—even more than 750 words at a gulp—and former columnists can get involved in causes that require something more than a keyboard.

Looking forward and backward, it is never easy to know the right moment to step onto that next stage. At a farewell lunch—which I described as the "sheet cake lunch"—my editor and friend read aloud some vaguely familiar words by a columnist 30 years my junior.

"There's a trick to the Graceful Exit. It begins with the vision to recognize when a job, a life stage, a relationship is over—and to let go. It means leaving what's over without denying its validity or its past importance in our lives.

"It involves a sense of future, a belief that every exit line is an entry, that we are moving on rather than out."

It was an odd experience to hear, let alone heed, my younger self.

"The trick of retiring well may be the trick of living well," I wrote back then. "It's hard to recognize that life isn't a holding action, but a process. It's hard to learn that we don't leave the best parts of ourselves behind, back in the dugout or the office. We own what we learned back there. The experiences and the growth are grafted onto our lives. And when we exit, we can take ourselves along—quite gracefully."

She knew then what I know much more intimately now. So, with her blessing, I will let myself go. And go for it.

"Vigorous writing is concise."
- William Strunk, Jr. *The Elements of Style*

MARK HOPKINS

Saying More in Less than 450 Words

Less must be more because editors no longer accept 1,000+ word op-ed columns. Although 750-word columns are typical, some editors press for 500 words because of shrinking print space and the shorter attention span of readers. The challenge, therefore, is to convey a brief, but powerful message.

Despite the unlimited space for Internet pieces, long paragraphs or sentences rarely benefit a public issue. How often has one temporarily set aside a lengthy piece never to return to it? Conciseness focuses the reader's attention and wastes no time.

One columnist makes do with 450 words or fewer. "The necessity of writing shorter columns makes one a better writer," said syndicated columnist Mark Hopkins whose columns appear three times a month in *The Anderson (S.C.) Independent-Mail*, on Scripps.com and for GateHouse Media. His book, *Facts & Opinions On the Issues of Our Times,* is a collection of opinion pieces in which history, humor and statistics advance his ideas within space constraints.

According to Hopkins, the challenge of a limited word count is in knowing "how to give a complete picture of a topic and still pare it down to fit within a column space the editor has available for you."

Mark Hopkins' Writing Process, Insights, and Advice

To create writing that is compact with impact, Hopkins advises:

<u>Have a clearly defined purpose</u>. Your opinion must have an affirmative purpose, one with a definable outcome that will provide information and better understanding. Does your audience understand global warming, the ramifications of the new health care law, or the issues related to illegal immigration? If not, how can you help? If you know your purpose, then creating clarity within your column becomes much easier.

<u>Limit the points you want to make, make them, and quit</u>. Your editor has given you a word count. Most people can absorb three ideas at a time, so narrow your arguments to three or fewer that drive your message home. Avoid digression. Stay on point.

<u>Assume the reader has the basic facts</u>. When writing a 450-word column, assume your readers know the basics of an issue and are searching for new information or a fresh perspective on a particular subject. Give your reader credit for being discerning, capable of forming opinions, and taking action on those opinions. In short, you don't have to spell everything out for the reader. Fight the urge to over explain the issues.

<u>Make it memorable</u>. Use drama, humor, situations, or anecdotes. Readers are more likely to remember stories than statistics. Let your subject and your points carry the column. Avoid using too many adjectives. Instead, employ active verbs and vivid imagery.

Abbreviated writing can excite the imagination and senses. The goal is to generate rich prose, individual style, and creativity within a limited space. Words live and breathe whenever the writing has rhythm, cadence and timing. Listen for the life beat of your writing by reading it aloud. It's easier to hear repetitive words, run-on sentences or awkward construction. As a public speaker and former president of four colleges, Hopkins understands how humor and the poetic use of words can bring diverse communities together for a common cause. There are lessons from public speaking that can be applied to writing.

"Writing a column is not unlike doing a three-minute speech designed to deliver a message or make a point. A speaker has a visual advantage, and the challenge to the writer is how to paint pictures with words that stand out in the same way," he said.

Humor plays its part. Effective writing is not just about slashing sentences as Hopkins noted in two examples, "Mark Twain replied when mistaken reports of his death were circulated, 'I would like the readers to know that the report of my demise has been greatly exaggerated.' Twain could have written, 'I'm still alive.'

"Everett Dirksen, a former senator from Illinois, commented on the growing size of the national budget, 'A billion here and a billion there, and the first thing you know, you run into real money.' He could have said, 'The budget is too large.'"

Hopkins noted that the Gettysburg Address is a brilliant example of concise wording that moves both listeners and readers. At a time when public speeches ran for an hour or more, Lincoln delivered one of the most stirring speeches in American history that used only 272 words and was delivered in fewer than three minutes. He created soul-stirring, beautiful prose through word choice, rhythm, cadence and phrasing.

Hopkins pointed out, "'Four score and seven years ago our forefathers brought forth on this continent a new nation.' Lincoln could have said in eight words, 'Eighty-seven years ago we created the United States.'

"When Lincoln ended with '…that government of the people, by the people, for the people shall not perish from the earth,' Lincoln could have used 11 fewer words, "…that democratic government shall not die.'

"The Abraham Lincoln we have come to know and revere could not have written those sentiments any differently."

Whether a columnist has a writing style that is terse or meandering, the goal should be to teach the reader something new in a memorable way without being pedagogic.

Hopkins invokes the old Toastmaster's formula to bring home the message of an opinion column when he said, "Hook your reader. Let your readers know what you're about to tell them. Tell them. Then tell them what you just told them. Your ending should provide something that sticks in the reader's mind. That formula will win you a following and a future."

Pride in the USA

By Mark Hopkins
April 14, 2013
GateHouse Media

In Proverbs of the Old Testament it says, "Pride goeth before destruction."

Still, no matter where I go in the U.S. or anywhere else in the world I continue to carry a goodly amount of Pride in America everywhere I go.

Whether it is an earthquake in Haiti, a volcano in Peru, or hunger in the mid-east refugee camps it is the good old United States of America that arrives on site, "the firstest with the mostest," as my father used to say. In almost every crisis four out of five aid workers, medical doctors, fire and rescue personnel on the ground working with the people are from the U.S. Amazing!

We have our flaws as a country, for sure. Even now we have a homeless population of several million people and a full quarter of our children are not covered by health insurance. We argue among ourselves over what to do about both. Hopefully, Obamacare will take care of a part of that problem. One would think that a country founded on the nobility of sacrifice and the blessings of the Almighty could do better. But, just when we begin to get frustrated with ourselves about our own shortcomings, here comes another international tragedy and there goes an invasion of Americans who suddenly appear with picks and shovels, white coats and stethoscopes, hot food and encouragement. This didn't start just last week, though we tend to forget each time until the next.

Let's review. Who created for the world the United Nations that still makes its home in New York City? Note the presence under its umbrella of UNICEF and The World Bank who share benevolent services and money with countries around the globe? Who rebuilt all of Europe and Asia following the great wars? Who leads the world in providing humanitarian aid after earthquakes and hurricanes? Who created benevolences like Hospice, Red Cross and Community Crisis Centers all funded by local donations? Whose people give such great amounts in charitable donations to the worthwhile causes of the less fortunate? Who indeed? The people of the United States of America, that's who. The country built on the great ideal, the country that continues to fall short of its promise but is head and shoulders above every other that ever existed in taking care of the needs of hurting people around the globe. When the chips are down, you can count on Americans.

Watch the news reports. Wherever there is a crisis, there we go again, doing all we can to help against unbelievable odds. Sense the desire to help and the frustration of the failures, but feel the pride in country and a people who, once again, reach into their pockets and into their hearts to help those in greatest need. Can you feel it?

The Personification of King's Dream

By Mark Hopkins
January 21, 2013
Anderson Independent-Mail

From the Revolutionary War to the War Between the States to WWI, WWII, Korea, Vietnam, Iraq and Afghanistan, we tend to mark our time as a nation by the wars we have fought. No war has had a greater impact on our nation than the one fought in the 1950s and 60s for the civil rights of our citizens.

The civil rights conflict wasn't fought for military victory but, instead, for the soul of our country. The first symbolic shot fired in that conflict was by a diminutive lady named Rosa Parks, who cleaned houses for a living. She refused to give up her seat on a bus in Montgomery, Alabama.

The most visible architect of the civil rights movement was Dr. Martin Luther King, Jr. He fought and died in the battles that followed Rosa Parks' stand in Montgomery. It is coincidental that on the day we celebrate the 84th birthday of the man who told us he "had a dream for the future of America," we inaugurate a man for the second time who is the personification of that dream. As the King birthday observance brings to mind the turmoil of the civil rights conflict, we celebrate the inauguration of a president who is a symbol of the success of that movement.

America has its foundations in the genetic mixture of great peoples from around the globe. It is an expression of that foundation that we should elect a president whose father came from Africa and whose mother grew up in rural Kansas. What could be more natural for a nation founded in diversity and proudly called a "melting pot" by President Franklin D. Roosevelt?

President Obama has lived in the idyllic surroundings of Hawaii and in the daily turmoil of one of our major cities. He now has four years of experience in the crucible of our nation's capital. He should come into the fifth year of his presidency with a clear vision of American, not as we would like it to be, but as it is.

The theme song of the civil rights movement was "We Shall Overcome." The last line of the second verse says, "Here in my heart, I do believe, we shall walk hand in hand some day." The song advises us to put aside our differences and to reach out to our neighbors, to come together. If we do there is nothing we can't accomplish as a people and as a nation. There are no hardship too great, no price too high, and no goals we can't reach. If we focus on our problems together we can accomplish great things. We have proven it over and over. We can do it again.

"After all there is but one race—humanity."
-George Moore, novelist (1855-1933)

DERRICK Z. JACKSON

Intersection of Race, Sports and World Events

"I consider race and racism to be a beat, just like education, crime, or covering city government," said Derrick Z. Jackson of *The Boston Globe*.

However, this multiple awards-winning journalist does not focus exclusively on racial issues. "I'm 57 years old now, and I've been writing a column for 24 years. I think racism is embedded in a tremendous amount of issues, but I've also written a lot about the environment, graduation rates of college sports teams, and education issues from elementary school to higher education."

Jackson, who is African-American, believes his writing about race invites criticism, a common experience for writers of color. "Many times the points of view of black columnists have been challenged or editors try to water them down. Some [columnists] quit because they couldn't take the attempts to significantly censor their work. Newsrooms still remain disproportionally white, so there is pressure to black columnists not to bring the fullness of their experiences to their columns.

"Anytime there is a major type of racial incident, you can rely on newspapers to say it's the most vexing problem in the county, but if you write about it, it then somehow it represents a limitation in your work.

"Anyone who says he doesn't bring his life to the column is lying. All you can do is to write honestly as a columnist of color. Treat the experiences that bring you to the column with every bit of value as anybody else's," said Jackson who in 2001 was a Pulitzer Prize finalist for commentary.

When only 16, he wrote his first opinion. "I was working for the African American newspaper in Milwaukee while in high school, and I was watching a Little League baseball game. The parents were screaming at the umpire and becoming more like children than their own children. I felt compelled to tell them to calm down."

He learned early that a race-related subject could draw ire, even though the writer's intent was not to be divisive. As a high school student in 1971, Jackson was berated for 20 minutes by the vice principal for writing about Malcolm X, who had been assassinated in 1965. "I wrote two, frankly, pedestrian commentaries on the biography of Malcolm X, and I had stressed more the end of his life, how he had gone to Mecca and had come to the conclusion that the struggle for racial justice could include everyone."

Jackson recalled his exchange with the vice principal.
VP: "You're dividing this school!"
DZJ: "Who's saying I'm dividing the school? No one's telling me that."
VP: "I just know that this is very divisive stuff here!"
DZJ: "Do you believe in freedom of speech?"
The school official turned red, stammered, "Yes," and ordered Jackson from the room, a pivotal moment for the budding journalist.

"Mr. Bluster became a pile of jelly. I realized, 'Wow, I just froze the vice principal of my high school,' and it was a huge school, 3,000 to 4,000 kids. I stumbled onto something powerful—the power of the pen—and I've never looked back."

After his student years reporting for *The Milwaukee Journal* and *The Milwaukee Courier*, Jackson became a reporter for *Newsday* for nine and a half years and occasionally wrote guest commentaries.

Holding powerful people accountable was a significant influence in becoming a columnist, and covering a major story for *Newsday* opened that door. On October 23, 1984 Bishop Desmond Tutu visited Washington, D.C. and gave a statement against apartheid to the United Nations Security Council. An appeal was made to U.S.

corporations to stop doing business in South Africa in order to create financial pressure against apartheid. Instead President Reagan encouraged a policy of constructive engagement to which Bishop Tutu responded: "In my view, the Reagan administration's support and collaboration with ... [apartheid] is equally immoral, evil and totally un-Christian... You are either for or against apartheid and not by rhetoric. You are either in favor of evil or you are in favor of good. You are either on the side of the oppressed or on the side of the oppressor. You can't be neutral."

As a *Newsday* reporter, Jackson attended his first White House press conference, and asked President Reagan to respond to Bishop Tutu. "He acted like he didn't hear my question, so I asked again, and he completely did not address it. It made me want to do more than just report. I wanted to report emotionally with journalistic principles behind it."

The episode impelled him to pursue full time opinion writing.

Jackson and his wife, Dr. Michelle Holmes, relocated in 1988 to Boston, where *The Boston Globe* hired him initially as a metro columnist, and two years later, he became an op-ed columnist.

His life experiences form his outlook and inform his work. "The core thing is that I am an ordinary black kid from a working class neighborhood in Milwaukee who made it through and I want everyone to have the opportunities I had, great public school teachers, great mentors.

"I lived on a strong working class block where parents really looked after kids. College was ridiculously cheap. My final senior semester at the University of Milwaukee was in the high $300s for a full load of courses.

"I see a world today where the ability to live your dreams was slipping away in the 1980s and I would argue that today those opportunities have slipped away even more." Much of Jackson's early career was steeped in sports coverage, but his op-ed column today enjoys what he calls the "intersection of sports and real world issues." For example, "The Graduation Gap Bowl," reports the graduation rates of college sports teams, including disparities between white and black players. It is a feature *The Boston Globe* has run annually for 17 years.

"It's one of the things I'm known for, and its staying power is surprising even to me. I put out my commentary with the data. People look for their colleges and if it's good, they cheer. If it's not, they say they've written to their college presidents to find out why.

"The power of journalism is as much putting out facts and trusting the readers to be intelligent enough to make up their minds as it is telling people what they should think," Jackson said.

He has led his readers into deeper waters using sports as a venue. "Our society is heavy on sports entertainment and this was a way of having legitimate and important discussions on race, racism, and unconscious racism. It is far more engaging than talking about it in a straightforward political context."

In the late 1980s and early 1990s, Jackson wrote about how language in sports is applied differently to black and white players. After hours of watching and listening to commentators, he observed that descriptions of physicality—fast, quick, strong—were applied to black athletes. By comparison, white athletes more often were ascribed traits of intelligence, such as the abilities to analyze the floor, scan the field, move ahead, etc.

"My point was, if the most beloved black men on your team are described this way, then what's it like for ordinary black boys as they come up in the education system? If the most valued black men in society are being viewed to be more animalistic than their white counterparts, then that has to have a very negative, pernicious, subconscious effect on how people view black people."

Reader response flooded in. "When I did columns like that, you could back a mail truck through the *Boston Globe*," he chuckled.

Derrick Z. Jackson's Writing Process, Insights, and Advice

Find the joy. Jackson headed into journalism because it is fun and over the years his unique experiences included reporting at the NBA playoffs to shaking Nelson Mandela's hand. "I was a shy kid and very unsuccessful at dating as a teenager. Having a press pass made me feel like Superman. Just knowing I had an ID card from *The Milwaukee Star* or *The Milwaukee Journal* was like having super powers. I had hundreds of comic books as a kid. It's like journalism gives you X-ray vision into people's lives."

Aim for a novel angle. Jackson's goal is to approach problems in fresh ways. "I want the reader to take away a perspective that is either different from what they've heard before, or more sharply defined, or personalized in a new way."

Personal witness is powerful. Jackson has written about public transportation issues inspired by his travels to countries where the car is not king. He once attended an evening concert in Copenhagen, and, when the program ended at 10:30 P.M., he observed a woman in her 60s pull out a helmet and bicycle home.

When he visited Stockholm and towns in Germany, he saw bicyclers of all ages. "If you go to a country invested in making cycling truly a part of commuting, and you see the quality of life, it's almost night and day in respect to what we assume to be normal in the U.S. Part of op-ed writing is persuading readers that what they think is normal doesn't necessarily have to be so."

Know the point of your column. In 1979, Jackson felt intimidated when covering the NBA Championship finals. "I looked to my left at the great sports writers Larry Whiteside and Bob Ryan of *The Boston Globe*, and then I looked to my right at other greats from LA, Chicago and D.C. and I totally panicked and freaked out. How can my words compete with these guys?"

Plagued by second-guessing and stilted writing, Jackson felt despondent, especially when his lead paragraphs were changed and editors rewrote his pieces.

His *Newsday* editor, Dick Sandler, gave him a valuable tip on how to find the heart of a story: "Go through your notebook and then close it. Then write in one sentence the point of your story, and you only get one comma to continue the sentence.

"That piece of advice has always stood the test of time. If I have problems, I try to make it one sentence and one comma, and if I can't do it, I need to do more reporting."

Offer your point straight up. Readers are expecting an opinion, so they want the facts delivered quickly, according to Jackson.

"Marjorie Pritchard, my editor at *The Globe*, has more often than I want to admit disabused me of using fancier, more florid types of leads."

Tighten the flab and when offered constructive criticism, take it. "If you are going to be successful, have the courage to let an editor speak honestly with you about your work."

Former *Newsday* editor, Les Payne, was Jackson's most influential boss who demanded trim and taut writing. "Les' favorite word for me was flabby. That was a touchstone word for me because I was fat as a kid. Whenever he called my drafts flabby, I knew I had to tighten it up."

Be reminded of good advice. "I made the 'mistake' of telling my wife all the things that Dick Sandler and Les Payne told me. So on many occasions she has been my best editor, reading my drafts and saying quite bluntly over the kitchen table, "This doesn't make sense. What are you trying to say in one sentence?"

Reliable research. For source information, Jackson uses LexisNexis and observed, "Peer review studies are the gold standard for proving points when such data is available. Government statistics are good, too.

"In politics and social commentary, we are compelled to come to our decisions by using facts. Everyone has an opinion, but can you keep people interested for more than five sentences? You have to back it up quickly and effectively.

"My strength in research comes from being honest with myself. I start every column as if I know nothing. I might have an idea of how something offends me, or thrills me, but how do I back that up?"

Facts can't be beat. Jackson often receives emails praising his effectiveness as a columnist, and his use of facts is a key reason. "What seem to be plain vanilla facts are often the most powerful element of a column."

Jackson taught journalism at Simmons College for 10 years and developed a special activity to explore persuasive writing. He had his students read opinions on www.townhall.com, an aggregator of conservative commentary and then read opinions on www.commondreams.org, its liberal and left counterpart. Which side typically won? "The vast majority of my students would call themselves liberal. Yet when I had them take an issue and read pieces from both sides, they often felt the conservative writers were best because they used facts in making their points."

Put a premium on common sense. In the end, an op-ed columnist writes from the heart of his beliefs. "I come from a working class, family-oriented neighborhood surrounded by men and women who worked hard, and, even though they were all non-college people, they didn't suffer fools gladly.

"My dad used to say, 'Straight A's don't mean a thing if you don't have common sense.' More than I realized, that has been a silent credo for what I do."

March Madness brings vast graduation gaps

By Derrick Z. Jackson
March 30, 2013
The Boston Globe

US Education Secretary Arne Duncan did not dribble around the question when I asked him if collegiate basketball programs with long-term, gross racial disparities in graduation rates should be banned from March Madness. "Where you have insidious gaps, and where there isn't movement, I think there have to be consequences," Duncan said in a conference call on athletic reform last week.

In a follow-up interview the next day, Duncan added, "If a team can show it's improving, that's one thing. But if a team is in the same spot for 10 years, if your dropout rate is such that your graduation rate year after year is 30 [percent], 30, 30, 30, that shows you're less serious."

Duncan's thoughts, should he continue to voice them, could help move the National Collegiate Athletic Association to take its next major step to end the exploitation of African-American athletes. The NCAA took one meaningful step this year by banning 2011 national champion Connecticut from this year's tournament because of low longterm graduation rates. They were 11 percent for the entire team last year.

But UConn was the lowest-hanging of the rotten fruit in big-time college sports. There are many more teams that make a mockery of the student-athlete model. Many basketball and football programs have what appear to be acceptable overall team graduation rates of 50 percent or higher, but their numbers hide unacceptable disparities between healthy graduation rates for white players and abysmal ones for black players. The 50 percent standard was advocated for many years by reformers as the minimum acceptable standard for postseason play, but it is not adequate.

For the third straight year in the 68-team field, 21 teams had black graduation rates below 50 percent. They include Indiana, Ohio State, Wisconsin, Syracuse, Arizona, and the ostensible "public Ivy" California, along with small-school darlings Butler and LaSalle.

Florida was at the bottom of the barrel at zero.

The NCAA is thus far unmoved by the fact that nearly a third of the field is plagued by such poor performance, which is all the more noteworthy because most of those same 21 schools had a 100 percent graduation rate for their white players. A year and a half ago, I asked NCAA President Mark Emmert if there should be further consequences for programs in the tournament that harbor such racial gaps.

All he said then was, "We don't subdivide the teams by race or ethnicity or income. We do know when we've created and raised those standards, the graduation rates of African-American students have gone up sharply."

He was right up to a point. This is my 17th year of charting graduation rates for basketball tournament and football bowl teams, and a record 25 men's programs in the 68-team field for the NCAA basketball tournament had black player graduation rates of at least 80 percent.

These lofty ranks included former whipping posts of mine such as Nevada Las Vegas and Louisville, whose black players had graduation rates of 14 percent and 25 percent in 2006. Other schools that rose to at least 80 percent from 33 percent or below were Kansas, UCLA, Kansas, Creighton, and St. Mary's.

But the very success of those schools has created an even greater chasm between them and the schools that do not even try. Duncan's sentiments that the laggards should face penalties were echoed on the conference call by former National Basketball Association player and former US Representative Tom McMillen of Maryland. He recently reviewed the contracts of more than 50 football and basketball coaches in major conferences; he and Duncan coauthored an article in USA Today noting that athletic performance incentives in the contracts average $600,000, compared to $52,000 for incentives promoting academic performance.

Both McMillen and Duncan say that universities do not have to wait for the NCAA to act, and college presidents and athletic directors should make academic incentives a much more significant part of coach contracts. "It's a reasonably good suggestion to say there should be new sanctions," McMillen said, "and things like graduation rates should play a much bigger share of a coach's bonus. You don't want these pockets of disparity, but right now academic incentives are so minimal it's like tokenism."

The NCAA must crack down on the schools that try to get away with chronic disparities. Anything less means that, for all of the progress that has been made, the NCAA still is willing to live with exploitation and tokenism.

NCAA Basketball Graduation Rates for Men Based on NCAA Graduation Rates Reports of 2012

College	Black	White
Belmont	100	100
Bucknell	100	100
Duke	100	100
Harvard	100	100
Illinois	100	100
Kansas	100	100
Notre Dame	100	100
Pacific	100	100
Valparaiso	100	100
Villanova	100	100
W. Kentucky	100	100
St. Mary's (CA)	100	83
FL Gulf Coast	100	80
Gonzaga	100	80

NCAA Basketball Graduation Rates for Men Based on NCAA Graduation Rates Reports of 2012

College	Black	White
Wichita St.	100	80
Miami (FL)	92	---
Marquette	89	80
UNLV	88	100
North Carolina	86	100
NC State	83	50
Creighton	80	100
Louisville	80	100
Oregon	80	100
UCLA	80	100
Albany	80	83
Mid. Tenn.	78	100
Georgetown	78	---
LIU Brooklyn	78	---
Michigan St.	75	100
Montana	75	83
Iona	73	---
Va. Common.	73	---
Northwestern St.	70	---
Oklahoma	67	100
Boise St.	63	100
San Diego St.	63	100
Colorado	63	---
Michigan	57	100
Missouri	56	100
Cincinnati	54	---
Kansas St.	50	100
Minnesota	50	100

NCAA Basketball Graduation Rates for Men Based on NCAA Graduation Rates Reports of 2012

College	Black	White
Mississippi	50	100
Akron	50	67
Memphis	50	---
James Mad.	50	---
Indiana	45	100
Okla. State	44	100
Pittsburgh	44	0
La Salle	43	100
Syracuse	43	80
New Mexico	43	75
Colorado St.	40	100
St. Louis	40	100
Liberty	40	75
Arizona	38	100
Ohio State	38	100
Temple	36	---
Butler	33	100
California	33	50
NC A&T	33	0
Southern	27	---
New Mex. St.	25	100
Iowa St.	14	100
Wisconsin	14	100
Florida	0	100
South Dakota St.	0	57
Davidson (Not App)	---	100

A troop before its time

By Derrick Z. Jackson
February 02, 2013
The Boston Globe

Maria Henley of Cambridge was underwhelmed at the news that the Boys Scouts of America may soon let local chapters open membership to gay members and Scout leaders. "I can't stand up there and applaud," she said. "I don't think they deserve all this press for catching up to 2013. All I can say is that it is about time."

She could say that because she was ahead of her time in 1998, when two women wanted to enroll their son in Cambridge Cub Pack 56. "I said, 'That's nice,'" Henley recalled this week. "One of the women said, 'But we're gay.' I said, 'That's nice too.'

"I think they were shocked that I didn't say anything else. I'm sure they were so used to raising eyebrows, they kept saying things like, 'Are you sure it won't be a problem? We're two moms.' I finally said, 'I don't care if you prefer doorknobs.'"

The moms and their son were welcomed into the pack, in which I also had my youngest son. One of the moms told me in an interview for a column that year that the value of the program overrode the "horrible politics toward people like me."

That horrible era may end next week when the BSA national executive board meets in suburban Dallas to decide whether to let local chapters open membership to gays. In 2000, the US Supreme Court ruled in a bitter 5-4 decision that Scout officials had the right to strip James Dale, a gay college-age assistant Scoutmaster in New Jersey, of his BSA membership.

Since then, youth membership has plummeted to 2.7 million, half its numbers of the 1970s. The era of exclusion is ending less because of enlightenment than because of national protests, loss of corporate sponsors and the BSA no longer having a social leg left to stand on as it becomes one of the last iconic institutions in America not to acknowledge gay rights.

The rebellion began with leaders like Maria, 62, and her husband, Ed Henley, 64, who still live in Cambridge. While Maria ran the Cubs, Ed was, from 1993 to 2003, my predecessor as Scoutmaster. An appliance repair technician for the Cambridge Housing Authority, he echoed his wife's mixed feelings. Their sons Tim and Joey became Eagle Scouts, but Ed said the BSA's national policies turned them off from further participation.

"The irony is that Scouting is supposed to let kids teach each other and learn about the world, not be a little closed enclave," Ed said. "We're the melting pot of the world. Any kid who wanted to participate, we were excited about that."

By the time they turned the troop over to my wife, Michelle Holmes, and me in 2004, the acceptance of gay leaders and scouts was a non-issue. Our job was made easier by the Boston Minuteman Council, which had become the most prominent council in the country to write sexual orientation into its non-discrimination policy.

Since the Dale decision, the membership in Pack, Troop, and Venturing Crew 56 has been stable at about 60 youths. But countless families in our neighborhood and nearby schools never considered us because of the BSA's national policies. Even when same-sex parents joined our Scout groups, they were understandably suspicious of getting involved as volunteers, fearing bigotry at larger Scouting events—no matter how much we said that our council was a safe zone.

So while I am excited that the BSA may drop its gay ban, I share the lament of Maria and Ed, knowing that so many young people— because of politics—were never able to use Scouting to find themselves or discover that mountains, rivers, caves, and community service can go along with video games, sports, standardized tests, and Facebook. The same goes for the untold adults who were dissuaded from volunteering and creating the sense of community everyone says we've lost.

"Looking back," Maria said, "I'd like to believe we created an environment where kids could tell us anything. They knew we didn't pass judgment. You just give them a chance to figure things out. What has Scouting gained by putting kids on the outside for 20 years?"

The answer, of course, is nothing.

"There was never a good war or a bad peace."
-Benjamin Franklin (1706-1790)

ROBERT C. KOEHLER

Peace, Healing and Op-Ed

Robert C. Koehler is a self-described peace journalist. He ranks among the top op-ed columnists nationally, according to Media Matters, and the award-winning Chicago journalist has been syndicated with Tribune Media Services since 1999. His career spans 30 years as an award winning reporter, columnist, author and poet.

His national column is unique for its reverence for life. Koehler's opinions, non-partisan but forcefully political, debunk "might makes right" and he exposes the facts, motives, and consequences behind the propaganda of war. For example, he has written about morally debilitated veterans (PTSD, depression, suicide), the inaccuracy of drone strikes, the rise of birth defects in areas of bombing and heavy fighting, and he noted, "Peace journalism is essentially focused on the human condition."

For example, on issues of military buildup or foreign policy, the public often feels impotent, and a mindset of helplessness is what Koehler seeks to change. "I want readers to take away a sense of the complexity of a situation and a sense of empowerment. I truly am appalled at the idea of a spectator culture, where we simply sit back and watch celebrities, or experts, or events. I want readers to feel they are in the middle of a story, and they are empowered to each have a say."

His personal commitment to non-violence began when he was 11 years old. Fighting other boys was typical, even expected, but one day he hurt another kid and felt ashamed. "Fighting made no sense. I walked home, and I made a vow that I would never fight again. I never backed away from that and it became a fundamental part of who I am. I have a bad temper and it can heat up, but I work to keep anger in its place, and to not have it turn into anything irrational or violent," he said.

Koehler's first job as a journalist began in 1972, but he left it to become a homesteader in Michigan. In 1977, he returned to journalism and moved to Chicago to be a reporter and, later, the copy desk chief for Lerner Newspapers.

Today his work is syndicated by Tribune Media Service and is carried on *The Huffington Post, Common Dreams, OpEd News* and *TruthOut.* His work has received recognition and awards, and his career includes book authorship (*Courage Grows Strong at the Wound),* national speaking, and teaching. His columns have won acclaim through national, state and local awards from the National Newspaper Association, Suburban Newspapers of America and several Peter Lisagor awards from the Chicago Headline Club.

Koehler shares what informs his op-ed viewpoint. "I was always a spiritual person. I had a religion minor in college and I've always been open to all faiths. I was raised as a Christian and I think there's a Christian template in my beliefs. There's a human message in 'turn the other cheek.' I became a big believer in the anti-war movement in the 1960s and in the non-violent aspects of the civil rights movement."

The other key catalyst is his wife Barbara, who died in 1998 at age 50. Column writing for Koehler began with slice-of-life pieces in the lower end market of newspapers, weeklies and shoppers. Over time, his column evolved into political op-ed. "I lost my wife to cancer and I started writing about my teenage daughter and single parenting. When I married Barbara, I had been in journalism for years and I was drifting toward a journalistic cynicism. She re-awakened my conscience, and it was during the Reagan administration and our involvement in Central America that I became very political again."

In 2001, Koehler's work was added to an op-ed package available through *Knight Ridder Tribune*. "It was after 9/11, and I wanted to respond to what was going on in the country. I was aching for that and KRT was a great transition."

After his 2002 syndication contract with Tribune Media, his op-ed identity as a peace journalist became more dominant during the Bush administration. "I was dogging the war on terror from a peace perspective."

Koehler calls his columns "prayers disguised as op-eds" and the award-winning journalist believes it is imperative to examine truth from a spiritual viewpoint. Traditional journalism, which is focused on objectivity, essentially dismisses the spiritual dimension from a reporter's thought processes or as an area of concern to news stories. However, the spiritual aspect of issues is a very real component, and its expression will lead to the empowerment of others, according to Koehler, "Your voice and your conscience are one and the same so don't take it out of your writing. It's not the job of the journalist to hang onto the words of the powerful. Take corruption and expose it."

Robert C. Koehler's Writing Process, Insights, and Advice

Say what others do not dare. Journalists are watchdogs. Op-ed columnists have a duty to reveal new facts and to examine issues from novel angles. Often, the so-called "widely held opinion" exists more from a general reluctance by many to sound the alarm in opposition. The war in Iraq following September 11 is an example of how the media was cowed into tacit compliance, according to Koehler.

"Since nobody in power was saying anything against the war, it was against the rules to report anything in opposition. The media was helplessly stuck in what others were saying to them. I call it abdication of the fourth estate. It's how journalism loses its sense of mission. You cannot take a writer's voice out of the writing and still have deep validity."

Objectivity is a myth. Koehler believes one's feelings about issues do affect content, no matter whether the writer is a columnist or a reporter.

"There is no such thing as objective reporting. How you approach a story or organize it is still subjective. I used to cover the north side of Chicago for the old Lerner newspapers. I wasn't a columnist, I just wrote news stories. My opinion about public meetings was not the story, but I'd still have an opinion, and it would have an influence on how I organized the story.

"My answer is that everything is advocacy. If you pretend to take your conscience out of it, and let anybody in power to dictate the story, instead of using your voice, that's still advocacy journalism.

"I learned a lot about reporters who supposedly strive for objectivity. Fairness and talking to all sides are very important, but when you take your own voice out of what you are writing, you are at the mercy of everyone who is yammering at you. You deny yourself permission to have a deep reaction to what is being said, and you become a stenographer for the powerful."

To write well, listen well. Be a good listener to external sources as well as to the voice within. To understand what others are trying to say, first set aside assumptions, biases, and personal feelings on an issue. One's position will crystallize after the information gathering.

Koehler advised, "Be informed and know as much as possible about your subject. Later in that dark little place of just you and your computer creating the story, you will find your deepest feelings and voice about the issue. Voice is not about spouting off. It's about pursuing a story as deeply as possible."

Search for the answer during the writing process. Koehler doesn't always start with a sure-fire answer to a problem when creating his column. "Good writing involves vulnerability, the openness to uncertainty. When I begin the writing process, it's important that I don't quite know what I'm going to say. I find it during the writing process. That's where the vulnerability lies. I have a sense of the story, and a sense of right and wrong, but I try very hard not to be glib. I sometimes lapse into default certainties, but hopefully they are open to question."

Complexity is key. Nothing is simple, and disservice is done to the reader when various aspects of a problem are ignored. Complexity is one of the signature elements of Koehler's columns. For example, he wrote about a family judge who went beyond procedure to help a family through a bitter child custody matter involving relocation. To appreciate the resolution reached, the reader had to understand how each of the parent's needs and concerns contrasted, so Koehler distilled information from four different interviews. In comparison, many writers in such a case choose to play up the acrimony and feuding instead.

"It's abuse when you're just going for titillation. I try to convey complexity, and various things can be part of that. I try to write compellingly. I'm a big believer in a killer lead, and you get pulled paragraph to paragraph through the story. Any writer worth his salt will have some skill at doing that."

<u>A big ego has little credibility</u>. Serving two masters is impossible, such as the conflict between writing a no-holds-barred opinion versus being friendly with the famous. Koehler deplores the celebrity journalist because the writer's ability to bring the powerful to account is compromised, and he said, "As they rose in the ranks of celebrity, they became more useless as journalists, and became more like stenographers to the powerful. It trends in that direction."

Today, Koehler's op-ed column is evolving. Peaceful solutions apply to all aspects of life and he does not want his writing efforts to be associated solely with matters of war or militarization.

In a 2010 *OpEd News* interview, he told Joan Brunwasser, "To be a peace journalist means to plunge deeply into a topic, to let go of prejudices, to listen to people with sympathy and respect, and to stand firmly for nonviolent, healing-focused solutions to conflict."

The Buzzing Wasps

By Robert C. Koehler
September 27, 2012
Tribune Media Services

Somewhere between predatory self-interest and insanity lies the drone.

The war on terror, the testing ground for drone technology, may be no more than the threshold of a brand new, barely imagined form of human hell: hell that buzzes like a wasp. How long before the technology comes home to our own neighborhoods?

An exhaustive new study released this week—"Living Under Drones: Death, Injury and Trauma to Civilians From U.S. Drone Practices in Pakistan," livingunderdrones.org, a collaborative research effort by the New York University and Stanford schools of law—rebuts pretty much every argument drone proponents, including the Obama administration and Republican challenger Mitt Romney, have made for their continued and extensive use. They kill lots of civilians and very few "high-level targets," stir continuous animosity against the United States and thus guarantee steady recruitment by "violent non-state armed groups." They don't keep us safe. They prolong the war.

Their use is so illogical one has to wonder whether prolonging the war isn't maybe the point. Without hypothesizing a secret, shadow government that actually pulls the strings, I can imagine the self-delusion of present and future Beltway politicians, convinced with all their hearts that the "war on terror" is noble and necessary even as profits from it accrue to their friends and benefactors. The best way to wage a war without end is not to realize that's what you're doing.

"Living Under Drones" makes it harder to maintain that illusion. The book-length study involved nine months of research, two trips to Pakistan and more than 130 interviews with drone experts as well as victims and witnesses to U.S. drone strikes. The project began in December 2011, when the British human rights organization Reprieve contacted Stanford's International Human Rights and Conflict Resolution Clinic, suggesting it conduct an independent investigation into the effects of drone warfare. NYU later joined the project.

The study's primary contribution isn't in resolving the endlessly disputed data over "insurgent" vs. civilian deaths from drone attacks. There will probably never be agreement on such numbers. Relying on work by The Bureau of Investigative Journalism, it puts the number of Pakistanis killed in drone strikes from June 2004 to mid-September 2012 as between 2,562 and 3,325, listing 474 to 881 of them as civilians—i.e., innocent bystanders—with 176 of them children. However, only an estimated two percent of those killed were "high-level targets," according to the study.

But such numbers are mere abstractions, emotionally meaningless—how many Pakistani children are we allowed to kill in the name of peace?—without some accompanying depiction of the human suffering America's videogame war is causing. "Living Under Drones" brings home just that, making clear that the suffering is widespread and profound. With our 24-7 drone surveillance of the region, we're terrorizing the entire population of Waziristan, some 800,000 people.

From the executive summary: "U.S. drone strike policies cause considerable and under-accounted-for harm to the daily lives of ordinary civilians, beyond death and physical injury. Drones hover 24 hours a day over communities in northwest Pakistan, striking homes, vehicles, and public spaces without warning. Their presence terrorizes men, women, and children, giving rise to anxiety and psychological trauma among civilian communities."

Indeed, the drones "emit an eerie sound, earning them the name bangana (buzzing wasp)," writes Reprieve founder Clive Stafford Smith, www.commondreams.org/view/2012/09/25-2, who compares the U.S. terror campaign in Waziristan to the Nazi V1 blitz of

London during World War II.

And it gets worse: "The U.S. practice of striking one area multiple times," the executive summary continues, "and evidence that it has killed rescuers, makes both community members and humanitarian workers afraid or unwilling to assist injured victims.

"Some community members shy away from gathering in groups, including important tribal dispute-resolution bodies, out of fear that they may attract the attention of drone operators. Some parents choose to keep their children home, and children injured or traumatized by strikes have dropped out of school. Waziris told our researchers that the strikes have undermined cultural and religious practices related to burial, and made family members afraid to attend funerals."

And, oh yeah: "One major study shows that 74 percent of Pakistanis now consider the U.S. an enemy."

Let's pause a moment here and reflect on the multiple-strike policy: taking out a target with a Hellfire missile, waiting a few minutes—the injured begin screaming for help—then blasting the same spot with another missile. Could there be a crueler, more hellish way to torment an entire community? How would we feel, for God's sake, if some distant superpower were harassing us in such a way? In such contemplation do I begin to wonder whether the policymakers have a larger end in mind than "terrorist removal"—that is to say, the maintenance of permanent war.

This is the "peace" we're creating with drone technology and the limitless war on terror: a peace that will always be under dire assault from those who hate us and want to make sure we understand that what goes around comes around.

A Gospel of Wealth

By Robert C. Koehler
December 13, 2012
Tribune Media Services

"I'm pregnant," she said.

Well, OK. She wanted $4. I could have done the "pretend not to see you" thing. Taking that option is part of life these days, especially in Chicago. She'd been standing in the middle of the intersection, trying to get money so that—if she was to be believed —she and her daughter could get dinner at the McDonald's on the corner.

When the light changed, she came over to me. I was out for a walk. It was a beautiful, cold December night.

This is what I'd been thinking: "We are not human beings having a spiritual experience; we are spiritual beings having a human experience."

It was a quote from one of my favorite writers, Pierre Teilhard de Chardin, and at times it feels true—such as when I'm walking through my vibrant, unpredictable neighborhood. Suddenly nothing is ordinary or banal, nothing is to be blown off. Oh, the humanity.

She was young, but had a raw, weathered look to her, as though she'd spent nights in parks or maybe under viaducts. Why not just keep walking? That's the sensible thing to do, but I cannot do so— cannot avoid eye contact—without feeling a wrenching brokenness in my relationship with the world. Most of the time I can tolerate this and I move on; but sometimes a curiosity, or perhaps my own need for an I-thou connection to the world, simply stops me in my tracks.

And once I give eye contact, the story begins. And the story is always about money. Money separates us. Without it we're hungry and homeless. According to worldhunger.org, one in seven American households—more than 17 million of them—were "food insecure" as of 2010. It's "the highest number ever recorded in the United States."

Yeah, something's broken. It's systemic, of course. I won't fix it tonight, here at the corner of Devon and Ridge, as a young woman steps out of the traffic and tells me how hungry she is, and so is her daughter, and she's pregnant. And her words are compelling even if I don't necessarily believe her. "I'm for real," she says and I feel for change—because I don't disbelieve her either—but I have only a few nickels in my pocket. I pull out my wallet. I have a one, a 10 and some 20s.

I'm rich.

This is what I sense in this moment, as she stands there looking at me, illuminated by the streetlight and the glow of the McDonald's sign. And nothing could feel more preposterous to me than to feel, suddenly, rich, when in my own mind I'm anything but. I don't want to be rich or, at any rate, to feel a divide between us based on the contents of my wallet. And I think about the presidential campaign that ended a month ago—about the convenient divide that money creates between "taxpayers" and "moochers" and the righteousness that instantly supplants any internal conflict we might feel about the basic unfairness of the situation.

"It is well, nay, essential for the progress of the race, that the houses of some should be homes for all that is highest and best in literature and the arts, and for all the refinements of civilization, rather than that none should be so. Much better this great irregularity than universal squalor."

Wow, universal squalor as the only alternative to a wealth chasm dividing society into fragments. This was Andrew Carnegie, writing in 1890 (*The Gospel of Wealth*). Earlier he'd talked about how, in the old days, "there was little difference between the dwelling, dress, food and environment of the chief and those of his retainers."

And furthermore, "The Indians are today where civilized man then was. When visiting the Sioux, I was led to the wigwam of the chief. It was just like the others in external appearance, and, even within, the difference was trifling between it and those of the poorest of his braves. The contrast between the palace of the millionaire and the cottage of the laborer with us today measures the change which has come with civilization. This change, however, is not to be deplored, but welcomed as highly beneficial."

Oh, the entitlement! The poorest of "his" braves...

These are the prejudices—the spiritual contaminants—built into the society we inhabit. It begins with the myth of civilization and the abundance of technology and art and fabulous entertainment and great footwear it bestows, however unequally, on all of us, rich and poor alike. The viciousness of the enforcement of this divide is hidden behind the glorious abundance. Without the inequality— without the rich owning almost everything—we'd have...drum circles and moccasins. You know, universal squalor.

What I do is hand her the 10. I don't know if she's telling the truth, nor do I have a "feel good" moment of helping someone in need. I have only a bemused despair, either that nothing has changed and she'll be hungry again tomorrow, or her pitch was a lie (or maybe just a form of advertising).

When I hand it to her, she squeals, "I love you!" And I watch as she hurries off toward McDonald's, presumably to have a feast with her daughter.

"Storytelling reveals meaning without committing the error of defining it."
- Joanna "Hannah" Arendt, political theorist (1906-1975)

DAVE LIEBER

The Best Opinion Writing Tells a Story

Spirited storytelling breathes life into op-ed. The column might be about politics, current events, or a global happening, but readers care about what happened to whom. It's about the human story first, and research and data are secondary. Emotional depth, range and vulnerability are required. For over 30 years as a journalist, Dave Lieber has moved readers to action throughout his award-winning career as a reporter, metro columnist and consumer watchdog.

Formerly with the *Fort Worth Star Telegram* for 20 years, Lieber is now with the *Dallas Morning News*. Revealing the heart of a story is his success secret, and this skill is vital to all genres of writing.

Perhaps many do not associate storytelling with commentary, but it is the winning ingredient among those with longevity in the writing field, and Dave Lieber is one of the best. As a national speaker and teacher, he authored *The High Impact Writer: Ideas, Tips and Strategies to Turn Your Writing World Upside Down* that features skills and techniques from his longtime career. Here Lieber offers his best strategies applicable to opinion writing.

To create commentary Lieber offers this advice, "Start with the op-ed point you want to make and find a story, or a person, or people that illustrate the point you are trying to make."

He observes that too many write at a distance, "People who tend to write op-ed think they have to be academic. They write bullet point columns, but a lot of smart points won't tap the emotional well of the reader. To be memorable, it has to reach people's hearts, not just their heads."

Emotional engagement is not touchy-feely fluff. Scientific evidence has proven that emotion is both a physiological and physical reaction that is sparked first from neural connectors in the brain. Writing that elicits a visceral response is memorable. It creates within a reader an urgency to respond.

Lieber noted, "The only way to get people to change their minds is to move their hearts. Franklin D. Roosevelt didn't give people bullet points, he gave them hope, which is tied to emotion, first through the brain and, ultimately, through the heart."

Many times columns that were not categorized as commentary per se made the leap onto op-ed pages because they moved readers in a very personal way using issues of the day.

Lieber's two favorite columnists are the late Lewis Grizzard of *The Atlanta Journal-Constitution* and Jimmy Breslin of *The New York Daily News* whose stories rang with universal resonance and deeply moved readers. Even though Breslin was a metro columnist, his work appeared on syndicated op-ed pages. "That's what got him on the op-ed pages. He fit because he told strong stories with a moral point of view," Lieber said.

Over the years, changes in the industry have caused a decline in the quality of op-ed. Increasingly corporatized newspapers prefer to pop the branded voices (conservative, liberal) of syndicated columnists into a publication's format. Too often, local writers lack the courage or the experience to swing hard in the ring. "Lots of community columnists are immature writers who don't have the skills," Lieber observed.

However, for those columnists who are passionate about the human condition, a place in history may await them. Lieber shared an example, "One of the greatest op-ed columnists was Ralph McGill of *The Atlanta Constitution*. He basically told the segregated South they needed to integrate. We still remember him."

Ralph McGill won a Pulitzer Prize in 1959. At the time, McGill was nationally syndicated and was one of few editors of a major white Southern newspaper to write in favor of integration. He covered the Greensboro sit-ins, a series of non-violent protests that led to the reversal of racial segregation policies by the Woolworth chain of department stores in the South. Eventually other newspapers followed suit. Commentaries written with heart will draw readers, but such writing remains a challenge to many. Lieber said. "Some columnists have this platform that millions of people would love to have, and they tend to waste it by being just smart and academic. There's a lot more to writing than that."

Dave Lieber's Writing Process, Insights, and Advice

The concepts of New Journalism opened up realms for Lieber in both reporting and column writing, and it remains the best advice of his career. In New Journalism, the writer applies the tools and techniques of the literary novel to non-fiction writing.

The four elements involve:

-Scene by scene construction

-Dialogue in full

-Writing from the third-person viewpoint

-Conveying the telling details that reveal a person's status or character

Legendary columnists Jimmy Breslin and Pete Hamill applied these techniques to their own work. These writing components are vital to creating stories that compel.

Lieber said, "It has brought me success. When readers tell me they love my writing, I know it is because they love the New Journalism. They love that I got to a scene early, before it unfolded. They love that I used dialogue to establish character. They love that I gave them a story with a plot and a climax. But they don't realize any of this. They just know that they loved the writing. And that's all that matters."

Basic Gear For Crafting The Story

New Journalism techniques are featured In *The High Impact Writer* where Lieber wrote: "We don't want to begin our tales with descriptions, overviews, or an analysis of the social problem. We want to begin with people, people, people who we care about. We care about them enough so what happens to them actually means something to us. That means that you have to take a press release or a news trend story from another newspaper and find a family or an individual in your community who is undergoing the same, well, hero's journey with all the attendant ups and downs."

Use stories to frame your op-ed argument. As an example, Lieber refers to the national issue of obesity. Instead of statistics, introduce "Angelina," an overweight schoolgirl. (Real names do not have to be used). Evoking emotion (for example, empathy, compassion, even anger or repulsion) will get readers to think about kids they know. Many may recall personal struggles or taunts from their own childhoods. Readers will identify more with a person who wrestles with an issue, than they will with current findings.

Bring the reader into the experience. As a way to gather facts and details that "show, don't tell," reach out and connect with those familiar with obesity to find out what a child experiences. For example, call the school district's nutritionist to find out how "Angelina" is affected in everyday life. What names do the kids call her? How is she treated? What do other kids do to her? Include a moving quote from the nutritionist. The reader then becomes invested in what happens. Lieber said, "You need quotes and dialogue to build characters instead of writing, for example, '40 percent of Americans do this or that.'"

Writing about the unfamiliar? Not well versed on a topic? Lieber suggests a full-proof solution, "Ask. Too many writers are afraid to go out and learn, to see for themselves, or to ask questions before they write about their subject, especially op-ed columnists. Too often they are tied to their desks, reading about studies and think tanks to build their columns. With three or four extra phone calls they would get a story about what the research is about."

To convey emotion, the writer must feel it personally, so pay witness. Invest your heart, otherwise a story fueled only by data will be forgotten. "Statistics are not only secondary, they are tertiary. I can always tell when a writer never leaves his office," Lieber said.

Op-Ed as Opera

Good storytelling crosses into all genres of writing and op-ed is no exception. Lieber is critical of dull commentary, and said, "The op-ed page tends to be serious, dry and predictable. Many columnists tend to write for the elite 10 percent and are too academic for the regular reader, but newspapers are the last 'everyman' medium in America. Anyone can pick up the paper and they ought to be able to understand it. Storytelling breaks out of the predictability associated with op-ed."

Writing a column is like staging an opera, and here's a quick summary of the three acts, in which the four elements of New Journalism have starring roles.

The Overture: The writer presents his topic. Just as the first musical strains captivate the listener before the curtain goes up, the headline and opening paragraphs of a column must engage a reader. This is the place to get personal when introducing a situation. The goal is to stoke the reader's curiosity. Lieber offers two sample openers. Which one would draw you in?

What began as a bright day in sunny Boston would be remembered as the worst day when a tractor-trailer slammed into a schoolyard full of children.
Or,
Accidents near schools are becoming more common according to a recent AAA study.

The lead introduces the issues and those involved, and vivid scenes engage the reader. When introducing a main character, use revealing details such as mannerisms or clothing to convey attitude or status.

The Conflict: The middle of an op-ed column is similar to the meaty part of an opera, and is the most important part of the story. It defines the hero, the villain and the conflict between them. The story comes to a head and this is to place to detail opposition, dilemmas or weaknesses. Against what forces, both within and without, does the hero battle? Put the reader right into the action by a skillful use of dialogue.

Lieber said, "We learn from failure, not from success. We can relate to failure. At the low point, the hero reaches into his pocket and pulls out the heroic attributes to overcome the villain. The struggle is not a straight line up. It's a jagged line because the villain keeps beating the hero down, and the hero keeps getting up."

The hero takes a beating, but don't club the reader. Resist the temptation to be heavy-handed. Subtlety is part of the strategy. Lieber advised, "Take the points you want to make and hide them within the story. A spoonful of sugar helps the medicine go down." How is this done? Instead of a litany of statistics, rants or pronouncements, tell a story that captivates and compels. The reader (hopefully!) will feel the desperation of the situation and becomes invested in how it all turns out.

The Resolution: At the climax of the story, the ending should cycle back smoothly to tie in with the beginning premise. Ideally, the column imparts a strong point of view, a lesson or call to action through memorable storytelling.

This type of writing is not for everyone because it carries an all-or-nothing quality of passion and vulnerability. Lieber said, "It takes a very special writer to pull it off. Not every columnist is willing to take risks, to write every column like it's his or her last. It takes somebody who is willing to put his or her heart on the page."

"Truth is truth to the end of reckoning."
-William Shakespeare (*Measure for Measure*)

MICHAEL R. MASTERSON

Investigative Op-Ed and Higher Purpose

Michael Rue Masterson offers daunting advice: be relentless in telling the truth. He places a premium on the power of intangibles, such as intuition, a higher power and purpose. He believes his career success provides convincing evidence that such things are real.

Prior to his writing op-ed for *The Arkansas Democrat Gazette* in 2001, Masterson had been a reporter for *The Los Angeles Times*, *The Chicago Sun Times* and *The Arizona Republic* where he headed that paper's investigation team. He later built an award-winning reputation as an opinion columnist who successfully battled institutional corruption. Yet, he does not give primary credit to his longtime reporting background in this regard.

"One way to explain my unique career is to say I have consistently been led to evidence because I definitely believe in a higher power within the human spirit. The tips of injustice were revealed and once the truth started coming to light, I followed it, and it was pretty easy to keep pursuing it. I laid the facts as open as I possibly could, but it was up to the public and the people in charge of the systems to do the right thing and fortunately, in most instances they did," Masterson said.

Time and again in his career, it was as if an unseen force brought information his way, and Masterson felt it was in exchange for his committed pursuit of the truth. For example, one of his early column series in 1963 involved the case of James Dean Walker, who was shot five times during his arrest in North Little Rock, Arkansas.

A policeman was killed in the incident, and Walker, twice convicted and imprisoned for that murder, came within a week of the electric chair. Throughout the years, busloads of officers routinely attended his parole hearings to protest his release.

Twenty-one years later, Masterson found evidence that Walker never fired a shot at officers, including the policeman who was killed at the scene. The police had overreacted in shooting Walker and had left him to die. When Walker survived, a cover-up ensued.

Over time, Masterson's columns freed him. The Eighth Circuit Court of Appeals overturned Walker's convictions, and he was released after having spent most of his life in prison.

The strange thing was the seeming ease with which Masterson uncovered facts in many such episodes. "I didn't go out and necessarily dig constantly for truth in so many of these cases. Instead the truth often was brought to me. It came to me. [For example] People had been looking for the real killer of their son for years and nobody would tell them. Well, I made two phone calls, and all of a sudden, I had evidence of the murder in hand, and the killer was charged and convicted. It's like the facts had been waiting for somebody to open the door.

"My colleagues used to ask, 'Hey, are you using mirrors or what?' How does he pick these topics that end up getting convictions reversed, or killers charged, or cases altered to make them right?"

For years, Masterson avoided answering that question and explained, "You're trying to climb in your career, and you don't want to sound to your colleagues like some kind of fruitcake."

Before Masterson reveals his secret, know that he has been a journalist for well over 40 years. He spent the majority of them as an op-ed columnist and editor to three daily papers. After a five-year stint heading the Kiplinger Program for Professional Journalists at Ohio State University, he returned to Arkansas as editor of the *Northwest Arkansas Times* in Fayetteville.

In 2001, he became a columnist for *The Arkansas Democrat Gazette*, and now he writes three times a week as a correspondent. Masterson never sought national syndication or a return to the nation's giant news outlets, preferring to complete his career with his statewide newspaper.

"My opinion is that I have one of the best jobs in journalism here in Northwest Arkansas, having worked for some of the best papers in the country, and at one time some of the most aggressive papers in the country. But at *The LA Times*, a so-called 'writer's paper,' you're one of 400 to 500 reporters. The stories you do are sweeping overviews and often impersonal in nature. I'm in a place today where I can make a bigger difference. In a smaller environment as a columnist, you become established and your voice can carry considerable weight with the people and politicos."

His fearless opinion and news writing have earned Masterson the highest journalism awards. Twice he was a finalist for the Pulitzer Prize for national and specialized reporting.

His multiple honors include the National Headliner Awards, the Robert F. Kennedy Awards, the Heywood Broun Memorial Award, The Paul Tobenkin Memorial Award from the Graduate School of Journalism at Columbia University for fighting against bigotry and hatred, the Investigative Reporters and Editors (IRE) newspaper award, and its Gold Medallion representing "Best of the Best." Masterson also earned the prestigious George Polk Award and the Clarion Award for best column writing on a large daily paper.

So what is Masterson's secret to such an extraordinary career, notable for uncovering evidence in unsolvable cold cases?

="Until recently, I was reluctant to acknowledge what I'm telling you. In an early career, most journalists are striving to prove themselves and to get to the so-called 'big time' of our craft. So naturally you don't want to acknowledge things that people might interpret as seeing you in a different light outside of mainstream thinking and behavior. So I didn't talk about it for a long time. But I know exactly what happened to me over the past four-plus decades and why it unfolded in my career. It's because I simply opened myself up fully and asked to be used. If you ask to be used, it will happen," said Masterson, who is 66 years old.

As a 26-year-old journalist in Newport, Arkansas, Masterson underwent a profound experience. "In the middle of the night I woke up and I realized there was something, I don't know, I can only describe it as an intense energy swirling through the bedroom. I never felt anything so strange yet palpable, so I laid there and simply acknowledged its presence. I said, 'I can tell you're here all around me.' It went fully through me and literally filled the room. Then I said, 'I know you're here for a reason, so just take and use me for whatever that reason might be. And when it's my time to go just take me.'

"That's exactly what I said. Afterwards, it was like a dam had broken in my life and career. I was continually led to these incredible stories where truth had been hidden, corruption of the crime lab, innocent people in prison, two guilty people who had gotten away with crimes, a whole community that needed reform. It was just amazing as the list grew and went on and on and on."

Masterson believes each person's life span represents a limited period to make a difference. The greater good—not one's self interest—should be the focus of existence, and he said, "If you are fortunate enough to be given a column, where your opinion is laid out for hundreds or thousands to read, then you've been bestowed a weapon of sorts because nothing is more powerful or feared than truth. How you choose to wield that weapon is yours alone.

"In my experience, I acknowledged that which created everything we know and I basically said, 'Help me to help because you have provided the opportunity for me to be here and share the words.'

"You have this sword of a fashion, words and a spotlight to use on behalf of good, and by good, I mean for truth. And with that alone, you can actually make things happen. If you or anyone violates truth, then you also open the door to evil, and evil always expands as far deceit and a vacuum allows. History certainly shows us that."

According to Masterson, higher intuition is lost when integrity is compromised. For example, if a reporter who is investigating a wrongdoing discovers a friend is involved, then the writer may feel pressure to protect, cover up or omit damning details, thereby damaging the vital connection to intuition and truth, and jeopardizing credibility.

He said, "The side columnists ought to be on is the side of truth. Whatever you determine the truth to be is based on the facts, not your opinion, although an opinion can be true. If you have sources that are showing you what is happening, and you don't tell because you're afraid you're going to get hurt, then you've done an extreme disservice to yourself and to the people who trust in you.

"I'm a journalist with a low tolerance for injustice. That's been the case throughout my career. You could say that fuels my outrage and motivates me to action. Heck, I'm 66 years old and I'm still doing that."

Truth is a beast with teeth that a columnist is committed to unleashing. No op-ed columnist can be neutral when it comes to truth, according to Masterson, who coined an expression: "Evil flourishes in direct correlation to the extent that truth is violated." He added, "In other words, tell a little lie create a little evil. Tell a bigger lie create a bigger evil. It's a matter of balance. When you knowingly deviate from what is true for whatever reason—personal gain or attention—you create evil. Forget the politics of an issue. What really happened? Let the chips fall and balance will be maintained.

"That's how I see life anyway. I am a physical, failing shell. And it can fail at any minute from a car wreck, disease, accident or something. While we may be but a shell, the essence of who you and I are and what we stand for during our limited amount of time here rings forever through eternity."

Mike Masterson's Writing Process, Advice and Tips

As of 2012, Masterson is the top columnist for *The Democrat-Gazette* and now works as an independent correspondent, filing his op-ed column three times a week from his homes in Fayetteville and Santa Fe. He shares his own factors for his success and longevity.

Be unpredictable. Although his investigative op-ed has earned awards, Masterson resists being pegged, and keeps his columns fresh and unpredictable. A one note column limits readership, and can quickly grow stagnant.

"Predictability can be the kiss of death for a columnist. I have a natural bent for digging below the surface, so investigative columns come naturally to me, but I've mixed it up. Mine is a general interest, personal opinion column that can range from investigative to human interest, humor, local issues and matters that I feel people would find interesting.

"I recently wrote about awareness after death, does the consciousness survive the physical body? Tomorrow might be about the politics of Washington or Benton counties here. I've also had several investigative series as a columnist. If readers know where you're coming from, it strikes the same note over and over. Being predictable you can lose a lot of potential readers. You also can lose a lot of clout and influence because people tend to pigeonhole you. If you lock yourself into harping on a certain topic pretty soon only people interested in that topic are reading you."

Be tenacious, even when facing failure. "I've learned if you are trying to effect positive change or reform, you cannot quit. If the powers that be know that you have a reputation for quitting after three or four efforts, most of them will just outlast you. They might announce 'an investigation' to get you off their backs and then let that announcement fade to nothingness over the ensuing weeks. When you are exposing injustices, you have to stay with it. Be tenacious. If you quit, you are inviting a potentially crucial matter to fade into nothingness yet again.

"I wrote about the death of a 16-year-old girl in a little mountain town in Arkansas. The evidence was so clear there was a cover-up on the state level. The state was too involved in it to open it up again because it would come crashing down on them. But the truth was all there and I kept hammering at it and laying it out, and I wrote over 200 columns over four years. But even that monumental effort in disclosing so much truth to my readers across the state wasn't enough to force the system to do the right thing. Sometimes you do all you can do to cast light and it still fails to overwhelm the darkness."

Ways to get reluctant sources to talk. A columnist's good reputation bolsters a source's willingness to reveal information. "The strategy for me has always been tenacity, not to quit the first time somebody doesn't provide what they said they would provide. If you know something's true, then you sit down and figure ways around the wall.

"One way for me is to allow a source to remain anonymous in exchange for their help in getting the word to the public. I ask if they will help me to find a way to get to the truth without having to name them. I'll say, 'I've never given a source up after decades now, so help me to find another pathway to the truth; to information I can use so people who read my column can trust my word." Often, Masterson is pointed in the direction of key players in a case, which he confronts with confirmed information from his unnamed source, a tactic sufficient to set the truth free.

Trust your gut feelings. "There are a lot of things going on in this existence that we don't understand, and we won't understand with our limited senses. If you follow your intuition, you can't go wrong as a columnist."

In 2012, Masterson was awarded the Will Rogers Humanitarian Award from the National Society of Newspaper Columnists and he said, "It's presented for a compilation of one person's career efforts. It meant so much to me at this point in my life because of what that recognition stands for. To me it says, 'You've done the right thing. You've spoken for the people and the truth on their behalf.'"

An enduring and indelible stain

By Mike Masterson
July 26, 2006
Arkansas Democrat-Gazette

This is an open letter to Ron and Mona Ward of Marshal, Arkansas:

I write today before the eyes of our state to tell you how deeply sorry I remain that after 18 months, the powers responsible for finding justice for your departed daughter continue to disgracefully avoid their sacred responsibilities.

The case of your sweet 16-year-old Janie's brutal and violent death in 1989 is one of the blackest of inedible stains on this state and the criminal justice system that should be helping ease your anguish rather than relentlessly inflicting more upon you.

As you know, I have written well over 100 columns since October of 2004 in hopes that by exposing so many previously unknown truths and urging the relevant elected officials to finally fulfill their duties with integrity and honor, justice would prevail.

I regret those efforts and the resulting light have resulted no relief. Instead, what I told you when I began digging into Janie's death almost two years ago has proven true: At some point the system has to work to ever ensure justice is achieved.

Instead, you have been continually subjected to the indignity and disgrace of even more stonewalling by that very system. I can't begin to fathom the depths of your anguish and heartache as the parents of a child whose killing remains unresolved despite so many available facts.

It is inexcusable to me that the 18th Judicial West special prosecutor Tim Williamson of Mena has done virtually nothing to resolve this case in all these months. This, despite repeated pledges and even the prayer he shared with you while pledging to finally lance this chronic boil upon the face of our state's criminal justice system.

It also is a shame that you have not been able to secure more coverage of the injustice you have endured beyond my writings. Janie's death is a very big story, as evidenced by the fact that ABC News continues to prepare a documentary about what happened to her.

You know better than anyone how the circumstances surrounding Janie's death were cloaked from the beginning so to prevent the full truth from emerging. Several then-children of prominent and influential Marshal families were with Janie when she died of a fractured neck and other head injuries at that teenage party in the woods.

And you, above all, realize just how deep and wide this politicized case runs for such silence and shielding to continue all these years. People have been protected.

And you also have waited patiently for one of those at that party who knows the truth to step forward as a now young-30s adult and tell what really happened to your daughter that late afternoon in 1989. The fear of reprisal persists.

As a newspaper columnist, I have undertaken to stand with you both to help reveal the many facts surrounding your daughter's death. But my capabilities are limited to the words contained in this space. I cannot subpoena the known witnesses to Janie's death or place them under oath and force the truth into the light.

I can only write the facts I discover and my opinion of them and your sustained mistreatment. It has been unconscionable. Not even the lowliest of animals deserve what you as parents have endured for almost 18 years. I also know you have prayed continually that Janie's case be resolved honestly and honorably. Your hopes have been continually dashed.

In our discussions I understand, too, you have strived to find forgiveness toward those responsible for your child's fatal injuries and for the ones in office who have steadfastly refused to fulfill their sworn constitutional responsibilities.

That has to have been especially difficult knowing that you, Ron, also served honorably in the U.S. Marine Corps in defending the principles of our Republic that have so miserably failed you both in Janie's case.

You each have known since that terrible night in 1989 that Janie did not die from inexplicably falling backwards nine-inches off a rock porch onto dry ground, a shorter distance than the length of my shoe. That was a preposterous version from the beginning.

Yet the authorities not only bought it, but perpetuated that bogus account of her death.

Marshal is a small town. People talk, especially across all these years. You know exactly who was around Janie when she died. And you personally heard the detailed account from the state's former Medical Examiner of how her neck was snapped from being forced backwards far enough to touch her backbone. You also were shown the X-Rays of her broken neck that became switched and altered in the possession of the state, then vanished completely.

Ron, you saw the look in the coroner's eyes the night he showed you Janie's damp body clad in a dark shirt you'd never seen before and denim jeans that were scuffed and muddy down the front. You read the EMT's report that said her body and hair were inexplicably wet and littered with sand and gravel even down inside her panty and bra lines. You saw how her neck hung unnaturally limp to one side.

In short, you have known from that very night that something terrible happened to Janie, and the powers that be from Marshal or Little Rock were never going to help you find out what because of who was involved.

Then, in October, 2004, Dr. Harry Bonnell one of the country's most respected board certified forensic pathologists with no political secrets to keep or friends to protect came to Arkansas from California without expecting payment simply to try and help bring some closure.

His re-autopsy confirmed exactly what you had known all those years: Janie's death was a homicide at the hands of one or more others.

And when Tim Williamson finally replaced Conway Prosecutor H.G. Foster who had done nothing with the case for 15 years, you felt hope for the first time. Williamson came to a Marshall church and even held hands and prayed for justice with you both. You believed in him even when it became increasingly apparent over weeks and months that he, too, was not actively pursuing the case. Hope steadily died even though the hollow promises and false hopes continued.

And today here you sit in July, 2006, trying to overcome the might of an entire state that should be helping solve the murder of your child rather than fighting two loving parents who only have wanted justice for their sweet Olive Jane Ward. What parent wouldn't?

Please rest assured, the hideous malignancy that has become your daughter's case has spread into the criminal justice system and across the state into the hearts and minds of thousands of parents and grandparents who empathize with your suffering. Many hearts and minds and prayers are with you. They, like I do, realize that precious Janie could easily have been their own daughter.

(Mike would write for two more years and over 200 columns about the circumstances of Janie Ward's death until the special prosecutor after four years and a second exhumation closed the case having reached no conclusions as to its manner.)

Farewell Uncle Bocky, the Prince of Gilbert

By Michael R. Masterson
July 10, 2002
Arkansas Democrat Gazette

Jack Eldon Baker, the unlikely and largely unheralded Prince of Gilbert, has departed from this troubled world.

His hamlet of Gilbert, about 20 miles south of Harrison off U.S. 65, paused to bid him farewell last week at the snow-white little Christian Church and Osborne Cemetery.

Nearly 300 young and old gathered from as far away as Austin and Idaho. They came to remember the 61-year-old man with Downs Syndrome, whom educated doctors in 1939 said wouldn't live through grade school.

Yet he lived far longer, enough time to teach so many others valuable lessons of his own.

Most who knew Jack called him "Uncle Bocky," because that's what he called himself during his adult years. No one knows exactly why. But that really didn't matter.

It was evident from the eloquent emotions expressed over his casket that this simple man's simple life along the Buffalo River had brimmed with significance and mystical connections. His unexpectedly long life was shaped largely by devoted parents and townsfolk who showered him daily with the same unconditional acceptance he returned.

The magnitude of his loss was palpable within the overflowing church, as so many people bared the mid-summer's heat just to offer a final farewell.

One speaker remembered Jack as the "Prince of Gilbert." Others said he had been an "angel."

Yet another compared his open and loving approach to life with that of the Christ he so openly cherished.

While a higher I.Q. might help most people navigate the storms of life, the genius displayed by Jack Eldon Baker resonated from the cells of his tender heart. He intuited the place where genuine strength resides, as evidenced by Sunday school reminder he so unabashedly shouted out most Sundays in this same church: "God lives in your heart."

The Prince carried on his teachings in subtle but effective ways. Family members and friends recalled his daily walks in the middle of the street to the Gilbert General Store and Post Office. His mother, Lucille Baker, was the Postmaster.

She and her late husband, Noel, owned and operated that general store for many years. Jack was raised as the youngest of two brothers, Noel Jr., now deceased, and Dr. Bill Baker, the former president of North Arkansas Community College.

One by one, people at this service related memories of the unique man's huge "embraces for everyone and his hugs that lasted five minutes." They spoke tenderly of the gibberish language that flowed from deep within his heart.

It delighted The Prince for people to hand him $1 bills. But, of course, he was especially fond of the ones with a five inscribed on the front. He called those fivers the "big boys."

Jack often expressed himself by creating patchwork artwork on paper with colorful Magic Marker felt pens. And he even sold some of that artwork for several "big boys."

He enjoyed watching the Atlanta Braves on TV and once met Hank Aaron during a game. But mainly his life was at home, the store, the post office and floating in the waters of the adjacent river.

Jack truly never met a stranger. And he proudly claimed he had gone to school with virtually everyone he met, regardless of their age. The Prince especially loved hot summers when he could swim and float on his back in the clear, cold waters of the Buffalo. Others relished his hilarious impersonations of Elvis, or the times he donned a Santa suit at Christmas.

All who knew The Prince perhaps were most moved by his endearing displays of affection, which also had to have encouraged his body to sustain itself for a remarkable 61 years.

I was struck by the realization that in 1939 had Jack Eldon Baker lived anywhere other than this closely knit community founded in the late 1800s on 20 acres, he may well have been institutionalized, or spent an abbreviated life in loneliness.

Instead, in an act that everyone here agrees was divine providence and a "perfect synergy," Jack was given a supportive family, a community to love and the community, in turn, was given its beloved Prince.

Jack attended the sixth grade in nearby St. Joe and did stay briefly at the Children's Colony for children with disabilities in Conway before returning to his family.

He later would tell his mother how, whenever he needed to weep at the Colony, "he went out behind the building to cry." At the facility, he also learned to write his name, but could never master any of the higher congantive skills.

Throughout Jack's lifetime, especially after 89-year-old Lucille lost her husband in 1982 and her middle son two years ago, she told friends that she prayed to live just a single breath longer than did her prince.

Lucille never wanted him to be without a parent, or become a burden on anyone outside the family. Last week, Lucille, her prayers answered, sat surrounded by the many who today care for her. In that sanctuary, she was thanked from the pulpit for giving the community the rare gift of her youngest son.

Members of the Baker extended family are the first to say that Jack shaped his core around unconditional love. "He never harmed or said a cross word to anyone," said Lucille. "And I never had to say a cross word to him."

Unlike many with far more resources who spend their lifetimes searching for purpose and meaning, the Prince of Gilbert was born with such secrets encoded in his heart.

He openly shared these lessons he fully understood with everyone he met: Love one another, don't hurt others, enjoy life, be open and honest, assume and celebrate the goodness in anyone else.

This man who fervently prayed for an hour each day, you see, never had personal agendas for personal advantage or gain at the expense of another. And what a remarkably positive difference he made in so many lives far beyond this little village.

The Prince drew his final breath at the North Arkansas Regional Medical Center in Harrison last weekend after suffering a heart attack in his bathroom at Gilbert that morning. And what a truly magnificent breath it was.

Ray Wheeler was seated beside him at that moment. "He just let the breath out slowly and this incredibly peaceful smile filled his face. It was an amazing thing to witness."

"I have come to the conclusion that politics are too serious a matter to be left to the politicians."
-Charles De Gaulle (1890-1970)

CLARENCE PAGE

Politics and Transformation Over Time

Pulitzer Prize winning columnist Clarence Page describes himself as a "liberal columnist who will surprise you sometimes" and he said, "I do lean left, but at the same time I reserve the privilege and the right to change my mind. What matters to me is to be able to give people help in forming their own opinions. I follow the headlines. I look at breaking news, the big issues right now on people's minds to which I can give perspective."

Page began as a newspaper reporter for the *Chicago Tribune* in 1969, which included a foreign correspondent stint in South Africa, running the city desk as one of six city editors, and a leave of absence when he served in the Army. In 1980 he left *The Tribune* to work for the CBS-owned Channel 2 in Chicago. In 1984, at the age of 37 he was invited back to the *Chicago Tribune* to be a member of its editorial board. "I saw my opportunity to get a column and I said, 'Well, if you could let me have a couple of columns a week, you've got a deal.'"

In 1987 his columns were syndicated by Tribune Media Services, and in 1989, Page won the Pulitzer Prize for Distinguished Commentary. In his spare time, very spare indeed, Page has written essays for the *NewsHour with Jim Lehrer*, appears on *The McLaughlin Group,* and has hosted several documentaries for the Public Broadcasting System.

Urban issues are his writing mainstay, a passion born from the upheaval of the civil rights movement. "I came into the 60s as a student and there were about 400 race riots going on around the country at that time. Dr. King and Bobby Kennedy were assassinated, the civil rights revolution was going on, and things were changing. That's where the action was and still is, for me, primarily.

"That thread is a narrative of U.S. history that says everything about how much the country has changed, and how much we are changing as we move into our multi-racial, multi-cultural century. That is my view," said Page who was born in 1947.

Civil rights and issues of color jumpstarted Page's early journalism career.

"I interned at the *Dayton Journal Herald* and when I graduated in 1969 I like to say that I was the beneficiary of a special kind of affirmative action called 'urban riots.' In those days almost all newspapers were not hiring reporters or photographers of color, but by the time I graduated they all wanted at least one that they'd have to send out to the ghetto," he joked. "I was the third black reporter *The Tribune* had hired in its newsroom."

While his earlier columns covered more wide-ranging topics, today his main focus is politics, and he moved from Chicago to Washington, D.C. to better monitor its heartbeat. Because his youth was steeped in social change, Page marvels that modern kids have little appreciation for the evolution of a society they now take for granted. Yet for Page, who was born and raised in Ohio, his experiences with civil rights will influence his writing always.

"For most people in this generation, it's just a TV show. The whole civil rights era is ancient history, a burdensome classroom assignment.

"I've always loved politics and for me politics has always been personal. I'm old enough to remember being a kid and visiting my relatives down South. There were white and colored signs. We'd arrive in the back of the bus, always conscious of the etiquette of racism. Even in the North, there were amusement parks I couldn't go to because I was black, or in those days, 'colored' or Negro. There were swimming pools in my hometown that were segregated.

"My first political feelers came when I was 10 years old. Those kids from Little Rock, Arkansas went to Central High School and Eisenhower sent in the 82d Airborne Division to escort them, and I watched that on TV. I saw that kids really could make a difference politically, a difference that could change our lives, and that was the first time I became politically interested."

In his columns today, Page observes a new kind of urban disruption, one that he feels young journalists should examine. Neighborhood gentrification, while successful in revitalizing areas, has caused property values and taxes to soar, forcing poorer residents to move out. Page recalled a conversation with columnist William Raspberry about the double-edged sword of neighborhood development. "The irony of being an urban reporter is that I came in during the era of white flight. Now it's gentrification and my late writing colleague Bill Raspberry said, 'We black folks get mad when white folks move out and we get mad when they move back in.' That's where we are today."

As a young boy growing up in Middletown, Ohio, Page had never set his sights on journalism. He wanted to be an engineer. "Growing up in a factory town, you get oriented toward industrial arts of different kinds," he said.

Mary Kendall, his high school English teacher, put the journalism bee in his bonnet. As advisor to the student newspaper, she encouraged Page someday to make a living as a writer. "I thought she was nuts. Mrs. Kendall was always talking about journalism, blah, blah, blah."

At age 16, he joined the student newspaper. "I wanted to have a social life and I couldn't play basketball that well. So I wrote for the student paper because I enjoyed writing. It was so easy but the very notion of making money at it seemed remote."

During Page's high school years, Martin Luther King, Jr. led a march in Washington, D.C., the Ku Klux Klan killed four little girls at the church bombing in Birmingham and John F. Kennedy was assassinated. "I was looking at the coverage of young people being hit with firehouses down in Alabama just because they were trying to vote, and it crossed my mind, maybe I could do this. I want to be an eyewitness to history. I don't want to be a slave over a drafting table, I want get out there and see what's happening."

Listening to newspaper reporter Frank Sennett during his high school's Career Day sealed his future as a writer. The day's engineering talk was full, but there were plenty of seats left in journalism. Rather than return to class, he attended the reporter's talk. Page was inspired, and he later majored in journalism at Ohio University where he worked on the college newspaper and wrote a column, "Page's Page." ("Pretty clever, huh?")

He worked alongside future bright lights, such as award-winning screenwriter Joe Eszterhas, Rudy Maxa of public radio's *Savvy Traveler* and photographer Ron Haeberle, famous for his historic photos of the My Lai Massacre in Vietnam. Page said, "I tell young journalism students that if you want to stay in this business, get used to the people around you because you'll keep seeing them the rest of your life."

In 1989 when Page won the Pulitzer for Distinguished Commentary, he rang up his high school English teacher to confirm that her yearbook inscription had come true.

"Mrs. Kendall, it's Clarence Page!"
"Oh, Clarence, how nice to hear from you."
"Do you know what you wrote in my yearbook?"
"No I don't recall offhand."
"You wrote, 'Remember me when you get your first Pulitzer Prize. Don't forget. Signed, Mary Kendall."
"Oh, well, that sounds like me."
"Back then you told me you thought I had a future in journalism and I thought, gee, that Mrs. Kendall says that to all the kids."
"Perhaps, Clarence, but you're the only one who took me up on it."

Years later in Northern Kentucky, Page met Mrs. Kendall's brother who shared that his sister always wanted to be a reporter, but in her day, girls weren't allowed to do that. So she became a teacher to encourage other kids to become journalists.

"Mrs. Kendall really made a difference in my life, so now I always accept invitations to come out and talk to high school kids."

With a career's longevity of nearly three decades, Page chuckles at the underlying commonality he shares with his audience. "I try to get a picture in my head of my readers and that picture has changed over time. These days I think of my readers as older, with more time on their hands, and they love to argue politics. Like me, they've got a spouse who won't let them bring it to the dinner table anymore, so they have to take it somewhere.

"I can't talk politics with my wife very long before she accuses me of practicing for a talk show. I can't talk politics with my son very much before he's trying to out argue me regardless of what the logic is. I've figured this out and it's only taken me over 25 years of column writing."

Awards received are testament to Page's writing excellence, but he holds some to be significant. "It's easy to say the Pulitzer, but the ones that stand out are lifetime achievement awards from the National Association of Black Journalists (2004), the National Society of Newspaper Columnists (2007) and the Chicago Headline Club (2013).

"What's important here is peer recognition. It's important to me that the African American community felt like I was doing something 'to advance the race,' as Booker T. Washington said. With my fellow columnists, to be honored is like the Oscar. An Oscar winner talks about how important it is to be recognized by one's peers in the industry, and it's the same thing with columnists. They thought enough of me to give me their award and to make me an honored speaker at their convention, and I couldn't help but to be moved."

Clarence Page's Writing Process, Tips, and Advice

"I'm best in the morning and my brain is fried at night, but thanks to my daily journalism experience, I can write any time, day or night. I'm good at writing on deadline, but I'm much better if I draft my column the day before. My wife accuses me of being an adrenaline junkie. Otherwise why would I constantly complain about meeting my deadline instead of writing more ahead of time?"

One's writing voice evolves over time. "It takes a couple of years of steady writing to begin to get your voice. After all these years, that was my biggest surprise as a columnist.

"My role models were Murray Kempton, Mike Royko and Jimmy Breslin. They were old-fashioned shoe leather columnists who would check the datebook [for assignments] in the morning, get out on the streets, and cover it firsthand. Jimmy Breslin was my favorite for characters right out of Damon Runyon, but Royko was my favorite for consistency. James Baldwin, Ellen Goodman, and Maureen Dowd all have distinctive voices and I admire them for different reasons.

"I saw how everybody else was writing and how they did it. I latched onto the styles I really respected. At first I imitated them, and then I put my own flavor on it."

Capturing a regional quality is a stand out asset, even if the trend is fading. Page said, "When you talk about Molly Ivins, Jimmy Breslin, Herb Caen, Lewis Grizzard or Carl Hiassen, what do they have in common? They are all writing with the voice of their region. They've captured the spirit of their part of the country, where they come from. They become the voices for their cities or states, whether it's Texas, New York, San Francisco, Georgia or Florida.

"That's what's disappearing now, and it was disappearing even before the Internet came along. American society is becoming more homogeneous. It's less local and more national and even though local is still the heartbeat of newspapers in the Internet age, our local areas are more homogenized now.

"Look at what surprised Mitt Romney and the Republican party in this last election [2012]. They had completely lost touch with America's growing diversity and newspapers have been confronting that for years."

Readers value a sense of one-on-one with a columnist. Page believes Bill Clinton personifies the ability to create a personal connection. Columnists can likewise benefit from that skill in writing, and Page said, "Bill Clinton did a better job selling Barack Obama than Barack Obama has ever done. Love him or hate him, Clinton is the master. How does he do it? I think it's because when he walks into a hall, no matter how big that hall is, everyone is thinking, 'Oh, he came here just for me.' The ones who are really good at it will project that feeling right away."

Simple Anglo Saxon words appeal to a broader audience. During the 2012 Democratic convention, Page was fascinated by a linguist's insights about language used in the speeches given by Bill Clinton and Barack Obama. Page said, "Clinton uses Anglo-Saxon words, whereas Obama heavily uses Latinate words, words that end in "ion," such as 'delegation' or 'administration.' Anglo-Saxon words are short, punchy, and very distinctive. Rock and roll is almost entirely Anglo-Saxon. In political speeches, if you want to reach a broad audience, use Anglo Saxon words.

"There's magic there. Clinton's speech is well-crafted even though it looked like he was up there, adlibbing. As a columnist, your job is to stay profound, moving people in a few words, so you have to admire this ability."

Broadcasting v. the written column: "Being a commentator on TV and radio has taught me the value of the final paragraph as opposed to the opening paragraph.

"In the newspaper world, the lead paragraph is so important, but in broadcast commentary, it's how you finish because that's what people remember. Learning that helped me to be a better writer when writing in a different media."

Learning from mistakes: "There were things I learned the hard way not to do again. One thing is getting too personal, which I wish I hadn't done on some occasions.

"I was more inclined to take more chances in my early days, so I'd fly off and try doing something really wild and different, and it just didn't work, but that's part of the adventure of being a columnist.

"Now I'm better at writing in my head beforehand. I have a better idea of what it ought to say and how to say it before I write it down. That said I still end up writing, rewriting and changing my mind as to how it should be approached."

Cutting back on information is a challenge. "We columnists are stuck with the tyranny of space. You want to make your point as quickly and concisely as possible, and at the same time, make it in a memorable way that is going to be different from everybody else. The business is more competitive than ever.

"I have the habit of over-reporting. You might have 800 words now, but it's better to be closer to 600 because news space is smaller, people's attention spans are quicker, and when you are syndicated you don't know who's buying your column and how they are going to edit it.

"I still have the tendency to report. For example, when I was at the Supreme Court on gay marriage, there were massive numbers of people outside. I talked to people, to characters, writing down what they had on their signs, I get all this material, and I wind up with three times more than I can turn in.

"I have to go through the agonizing process on deadline of cutting back. The biggest challenge of my life in recent years is making my deadline, much to the chagrin of my editor."

<u>Take the time to appreciate how far you've come</u>. Page said, "It's a psychological thing. As a regular columnist, you completely forget what your last column was because you're so busy focusing on your next one.

"That's how I am, always looking forward, but sometimes it pays to look back. I'll read an old column and I'll be impressed by my own use of metaphors, or colorful writing to bring out a point, or something off-the-cuff that years later sounds pretty profound.

"Writing can be like wine. It takes a while to mellow before you can appreciate how good it is, and a good column stands the test of time."

High court ponders: Is racism over?

By Clarence Page
March 3, 2013
Chicago Tribune

Sometimes U.S. Supreme Court Justices Clarence Thomas and
Antonin Scalia remind me of Statler and Waldorf, the grumpy old
cranks in the balcony of *The Muppet Show*—except that in the
courtroom Thomas usually lets his fellow conservative do all the
talking.

And talk Scalia did during oral arguments last week over the
survival of a controversial provision in the 1965 Voting Rights Act.

The case of Shelby County v. Holder could decide the survival of
Section 5, the provision that requires nine mostly Southern states and
some jurisdictions in seven other states to ask the Justice Department
for permission, also called "preclearance," before making any
changes to their voting rules or procedures.

The provision initially was put into effect based on the persistent
patterns of sometimes violent suppression and intimidation of racial
minorities voting in those jurisdictions. Alabama's Shelby County
appealed the case arguing that attitudes have changed so much, even
in the South, that the states covered in the law no longer deserve to
be singled out for special burdens of proof.

That's not a new complaint, yet the law has been reauthorized by
Congress with healthy bipartisan majorities four times in its history,
most recently in 2006. But Scalia, who made his opposition to
Section 5 pretty clear, shrugged off those votes.

He said in effect that lawmakers voted for the law because they
feared being called racists if they didn't.

And he said that as if it were a bad thing.

More pointedly, he brought an audible gasp from the audience when he said the landmark civil rights law now amounts to a "perpetuation of racial entitlement."

Never mind the congressional support, said Scalia. Congress is very unlikely to do anything but reauthorize the landmark legislation forever, he said, since politically the cost of voting against it would be too high.

Bert Rein, the lawyer for Shelby County, expressed similar sentiments, flatly declaring the disease of voting discrimination to be "cured." Like Scalia, he appeared to be in a rush to declare racism to be over and done with, except when he detects it in civil rights law.

Yes, we have come a long way in this country on race, as evidenced by the election of the country's first African-American president.

But, as Wade Henderson, president of the Leadership Conference on Civil and Human Rights, pointed out, it was ironic to see Alabama bring this case forward. According to court papers filed by the Justice Department, Alabama is second only to Texas in the number of voting discrimination cases it has lost since 1982 under another part of the Voting Rights Act known as Section 2.

That's the main enforcement provision. Section 2 applies to all states and does not require reauthorization by Congress, but it also does not require preclearance before states can make voting rules changes. Since it can take a couple of years for a Section 2 complaint to be processed, the damage of a tainted election can go into effect before the case is resolved.

But oddly unmentioned in court is another provision known as "bail-out." It allows Alabama or any other covered state or jurisdiction to apply to be exempted from the law's preclearance requirements after showing at least 10 years of good behavior. Since 1982, no jurisdiction that has applied for bail-out has been turned down.

No question that we've come a long way since the days when police dogs and fire hoses kept black citizens away from voting booths in Alabama. But today we have new voter suppression controversies over photo ID laws, long lines to vote and other impediments to democracy.

We also have new complaints about language discrimination, among other signs that racial conflicts are no longer limited to black and white.

In fact, at a time when non-Hispanic whites are a shrinking majority, it's a good time for everybody to reconsider the importance of preserving minority voting rights, whomever the minority might happen to be.

Rand Paul has lotsa 'splaining to do

By Clarence Page
April 13, 2013
Chicago Tribune

Within hours after Sen. Rand Paul's news-making speech at historically black Howard University, someone posted this new definition on the user-driven Urban Dictionary website of an awkward-sounding but quite timely verb: "whitesplain":

"The act of a caucasian (sic) person explaining to audiences of color the true nature of racism," says the entry; "a caucasian (sic again) person explaining sociopolitical events and/or history to audiences of color as though they are ignorant children ...."

Whitesplaining appears significantly to be derived from "mansplaining," which first appeared in a thoughtful, hilarious 2008 *Los Angeles Times* essay by Rebecca Solnit titled "Men Who Explain Things."

Urban Dictionary now defines mansplaining as "condescending, inaccurate explanations delivered with rock-solid confidence of rightness and that slimy certainty that of course he is right, because he is the man in this conversation." I am guessing that a woman wrote that definition. Message received.

Anyway, as an example of how whitesplaining should be used, consider Urban Dictionary: "U.S. Sen. Rand Paul whitesplained to students at Howard University," it says, "that a black Republican founded the NAACP."

Indeed, even Paul looked surprised at Howard when, after he asked if anyone knew that the National Association for the Advancement of Colored People had been founded by Republicans, his audience responded with a resoundingly impatient "Yes!"

"We know our history," one student shouted. Unfortunately, Paul didn't. He had to be prompted from the audience with the name of Massachusetts Republican Edward Brooke, the first African-American to be elected to the U.S. Senate by popular vote—and Paul still mangled it twice as "Edwin Brooks."

Worse, he expounded at length on the historically incorrect narrative that conservatives often give, that blacks left the party of Abraham Lincoln to follow Franklin D. Roosevelt's promise of "unlimited federal assistance," while Republicans only have the "less tangible... promise of equalizing opportunity through free markets."

Yet, even if you buy that oversimplified view of history, as conservatives with selective memory often do, Paul completely omitted a much more important sea change, the seismic racial realignment that followed President Lyndon B. Johnson's 1964 Civil Rights Act.

In fact, Republican nominees continued to receive sizable black support; 39 percent to Dwight Eisenhower in his 1956 re-election, according to the Joint Center for Political and Economic Studies, and 32 percent to his vice president, Richard Nixon, in 1960.

But after conservatives nominated Sen. Barry Goldwater, who voted against the civil rights bill, to oppose Johnson in 1964, LBJ won 94 percent of the black vote. No Republican presidential candidate has received more than 15 percent of the black vote since.

Widening the divide was the "Southern strategy" with which Republicans mined racial backlash to win white votes, first in the South, then nationwide. Some Republicans, like former party chairmen Ken Mehlman and Michael Steele, have been quite candid and contrite in denouncing such tactics, only to be shouted down by whitesplainers in the Grand Old Party's right wing.

In fact, "rightsplainers" more aptly describes Paul's selective view of GOP history, including his own. When he was questioned about his 2010 interviews with the *Louisville Courier-Journal* and on Rachel Maddow's MSNBC show in which he criticized part of the 1964

Civil Rights Act, Paul denied the charge. "I've never wavered in my support for civil rights or the Civil Rights Act," he said at Howard.

Yet, as videos posted on various websites show, he wavered a lot. He opposed the part of the act that banned discrimination in restaurants, hotels and other privately owned public accommodations.

True to his libertarian beliefs, Paul used the old argument that the magic of the marketplace would prevent merchants from turning away business. But, as an African-American who is old enough to remember having to sleep in the family car on long trips—in the South and the North—after being turned away repeatedly from hotels and restaurants, I have a sharply different view.

But mere ignorance does not deter the rightsplainers. They just keep on talking.

"Success is to be measured not so much by the position that one has reached in life as by the obstacles which he has overcome."
-Booker T. Washington (1856-1915)

KATHLEEN PARKER

Rising Above Presumptions and Labels

Kathleen Parker of *The Washington Post* is one of the top nationally syndicated columnists. She won the Pulitzer Prize for Distinguished Commentary in 2010 and co-hosted with Eliot Spitzer, former governor of New York, a show on CNN, *Parker Spitzer*. It all began with a column 25 years ago, and she said, "Back in the day, getting a column was a reward for writing well. You earned that position."

A baby boomer, Parker looks years younger than her age, which she insists is a state secret, and said, "I was carded until I was 40." Perhaps owing to her "prom queen looks," as one writer once described her, Parker's reader mail sometimes suggests an assumption of privilege. But Parker's success, in fact may be the result of her lack of good fortune. She laughs when she recalls telling her CNN producer, "I only look this way. My mother died when I was three and my father became a serial husband. I've had five mothers total. There was a lot of dysfunction in my family, needless to say—crisis after crisis after crisis. I left home when I was 17 years old and I've never been back. I've pretty much paid my own way.

"The metaphor for my life is a trailer hooked to the back of my car. More than once, I've hit the road without knowing where I was going. When I was getting my Ph.D. in Spanish at Florida State, I decided one day that I didn't want to spend the rest of my life teaching. I went to my major professor and said, 'I don't want to do this anymore.' Looking up from his book, he said, 'I don't blame you. Go out and do something creative'."

She hit the road and, without any obvious qualifications, landed a job at *The Charleston (SC) Evening Post.* Writing was her creativity. For about 10 years she was a reporter covering both hard news and lifestyle at five newspapers across the country, including *The San Jose Mercury,* where she lucked into a job covering the birth of California Cuisine. "I tried to get a column there, just a food column, but they said, 'We don't think you're ready'." Out of the blue, an editor called from *The Orlando Sentinel* and said, "I think you have a voice. How would you like to be a columnist?"

"As soon as I got that call, I was out of town."

There she wrote a column, *Women,* for the lifestyle page while *Men,* a corresponding column, offered a male writer's perspective. "At the time I was a single mother with a two-year-old, and I wrote about that a lot. The focus of my column was the focus of my life, which was often personal. I was very much home and hearth-oriented."

The Orlando Sentinel ended the separate *Men*'s column, changing it to *Men and Women* under Parker's byline. Thus began her evolution into becoming an op-ed columnist. She recalled, "Once they did that, it just naturally became about gender and the sexes. Once you get into that territory, it becomes political, and once that happens, you're headed for op-ed territory."

Parker was at the *Orlando Sentinel* for only eight months before moving to South Carolina in 1988 to get married. *The Orlando Sentinel* agreed to keep her weekly column on a freelance basis. In South Carolina, newspapers were not hiring, so Parker found other work, but never let go of her column. "I went into public relations for about four years, always as an independent contractor, but I continued to write the column, and write the column, and write the column. I think *The Sentinel* paid me $75 a week."

In 1993 Parker drew syndication interest from Tribune Media Services. "I entered myself in the H. L. Menken Writing Award competition because it was the only one that would allow freelancers to enter, and, much to my amazement, I won. The executive editor at *The Orlando Sentinel,* John Haile, was a fan and he promoted me with Tribune Media Services, which shared a parent company (The Tribune Company) with the Orlando paper."

During her 11-year syndication with Tribune, she wrote two weekly columns, which some newspapers, including *The Orlando Sentinel*, used in their Style section and others placed on their op-ed page. "Basically, I was trying to straddle this line and it was very confusing, at least to me. It took about a year for it to evolve into what it has become."

Life changed her focus from family to politics. "I was just simply mom on the spot, and there's only so much you can do from that vantage point. As my child grew up, I grew up, meaning my attentions became more worldly as his did. These days, though I write mostly about politics, I'm not passionate about who's up and who's down on a given day. I'm much more interested in the big picture issues, the deathbed issues, what we really care about. I'm riveted by subconscious motivations, what makes people tick, or what is driving a particular thing in a certain way."

The "conservative" label irks Parker, a designation that was imposed upon her because op-ed writers have to fit within certain slots. But any label would irk her. She frequently invokes her favorite writer, Walker Percy, who said, "We should repent of labels."

"It's a point of irritation for me because I wouldn't have portrayed myself one way or another. Now op-ed pages have to have this rainbow coalition of opinion, so you have to designate yourself as something. Because I was writing sort of pro-traditional family columns at the time I was syndicated, the marketplace decided that I was conservative. I was saying things that were fairly heretical at the time, such as children need both a mother and a father. That was just considered blasphemous to the sisterhood, of which I had always been a part, but suddenly I wasn't.

"I was simply expressing what I was observing to be true in my life and in the larger society, but it was not consistent with what was being advanced ideologically by the American newsroom. So I was an outcast in my own newsroom.

"Suddenly, I was a right winger! My good friend Carl Cannon, with whom I worked in the 1980s, said, 'You could only be considered a conservative in the American newsroom.'

"Labels are a plague on our political dialogue, I think, because very few people live one way or another. We're much more nuanced than that."

As a columnist, Parker describes herself as a generalist: "I'm not an economics writer. I'm not a military writer. I'm a writer about life, how we live it, and how politics invades our lives. Politics is the debate about the role government plays in our lives and you can't ignore it."

In 2010, Parker won the Pulitzer Prize for Distinguished Commentary. Her *Washington Post* editor, Fred Hiatt, made the selections for the entry, which covered a broad range of subjects, including three that dealt with abortion.

"My editor picked the columns that he felt were the best written and made the best case for my position. A lot of people said, 'Oh, she won because she bashed Sarah Palin,' but "The Sarah Palin Column," as it may as well be known, was from another year. I had three pro-life columns in the batch of 10 that won. (The Palin column, in which Parker urged the then-Alaska governor to reconsider her run for vice president, suddenly catapulted Parker into the national spotlight as a provocateur of too much truth.)

More provocative than her position on Palin (subsequently accepted as conventional wisdom) have been her columns on abortion. She is pro-life, but steers clear of Roe v. Wade.

"I've long taken a pro-life position without suggesting that Roe v. Wade be reversed. I try to make an argument for life, the effects of abortion on women and men, and keep the focus on Big Ideas rather the immediate solution to a difficult situation."

She is philosophical on the subject of awards.

"I used to say awards don't matter, and I think that's largely true if you don't win any. But when I got the Pulitzer I decided I was completely wrong about that. It's huge! It put air beneath my feet. It made me very, very happy, and I can't explain why. Maybe it's because I've been working for so long and some kind of validation is really nice. Most of us wretches don't get rich so recognition is certainly welcome."

During her career, she had turned down various offers for television shows. However, the decline of print newspapers affected syndication revenue, forcing her to examine other possibilities. Parker is a consulting faculty member at the Buckley School of Public Speaking. She shared how the marketplace affected her decision to host a prime time CNN show in 2010.

"I rejected it for years. I refused to be on television. First of all, I hate the whole concept of celebrity journalism. In a big way, I now know what it's like to have your own driver, your own stylist, your makeup people, and blah, blah, blah. I was very resistant to that for all the right reasons; I just wanted to be a writer.

"Back in the day, 20 years before the Internet, someone in my position would be making very, very good money because every newspaper had to pay me according to their circulation. Multiply 450 newspapers times X number of dollars times 52 weeks a year and you're pretty comfortable. Now circulation is in deep decline and the money just isn't there anymore, so I supplement my income with public speaking and the only way you get those gigs is by being on television.

"I was having drinks with Peggy Noonan and David Brooks, and Peggy said, 'Do we have to do TV?' Simultaneously, David and I replied, 'Yeah, if you want to eat. If you want to get speaking gigs, you have to be on TV.'"

In 2011, Parker left the show to pursue other interests.

What does she know about op-ed writing today that she wishes she had known at the beginning of her career?

"I wish I had known that I'm pretty smart and that I don't really need the approval of other people.

"I think the hardest thing for columnists is to trust themselves, to trust their instincts, especially when you're young. It's hard to be hated, and that, unfortunately, is part of the job. You're going to have to accept that—especially if you're successful.

"My friend Pat Conroy compares the experience to the crab pot. We're from South Carolina and we go crabbing, and you pull the crabs in and you put them into this big aluminum tub. Of course they all want out, but only one gets to the top. And when he does, the other crabs would pull him back down. They don't want him out of there. That's life in the land of op-ed."

Kathleen Parker's Writing Process, Advice and Tips

Have laptop will travel. Parker writes from Washington, New York, and South Carolina. She's an early riser. "I like to write completely fresh in the morning with nothing else intruding." After two or three cups of coffee, she often writes in bed, snuggling with Ollie, her rescued, blind, toy poodle.

She selects her topic the day before deadline - usually, but not always. "That said, I do grab the paper and read it to make sure there's nothing else that interests me more because I do want to write about the thing that is most compelling in that moment." Generally, Parker might spend about five hours or so in research. The next morning, Parker writes her column in about an hour. "That's the fun and easy part. The hard part is coming up with an idea," she said.

Why she writes. "There's something gratifying about the act of creation, which is something I get to do every day. At the end of the day, I have a product, something I can hold in my hands. 'Look, this is what I did.' That's very rewarding.

"The other reason is being able to voice my thoughts. There's a reason psychiatrists say, 'Keep a journal.' Writing is a great way to avoid the loony bin. It's like a pressure valve. Release those thoughts into the atmosphere and you're relieved of the burden. But the creative part is the most important to me. I would not recommend that anyone do this for a living unless you absolutely have to. It's really awfully hard."

Don't preach to the choir. "What I don't do is to make people feel good about what they already think they know. Nothing bores me more than telling people what they already believe and then saying, 'Ain't I great?'

"[Regarding issues] I'm trying to figure it out. I'm looking for the proper response myself. I'd like to think that I take readers along for a fairly pleasant ride toward a logical conclusion, and sometimes I'm surprised by my own conclusions."

For example, Parker has written against lifting the ban on women in combat. She wrote that female combatants face far greater risks in war and consequences upon capture. Critics may feel Parker is negating equality, but she is convinced many brush aside realities of the female psyche and physicality because they fear political incorrectness, and she said, "It's the power of appeasement. This particular column had me more passionate than many because the evidence is so clear that we're doing things for all the wrong reasons."

You know what you know. Statistics and research bolster a position, but life itself is an invaluable teacher. Parker said, "Experience tells us 90 percent of what we need to know. The key thing is to fully understand it yourself."

Column writing is like going to school every day forever. "Writing two columns a week sounds easy, and people say to me, 'Oh, you've got lots of time, but basically, you're in graduate school 24/7. You're always studying, always reading, always listening and talking to people. To be a columnist is to be hyper-aware at all times and, at times, it's exhausting! There's so much in-depth homework that goes into every column.

"I write 750 words, but if I were to put together the file that I needed to get there, it would probably be four inches thick based on all the reading I've done. Of course, I've been doing this for 25 years now so I have the benefit of accumulated knowledge. I have a pretty extensive database in my head as well.

"But if I'm going to write on a subject from scratch, for example, immigration, I might have to spend several weeks researching before I write about it. I want to make sure that I really know that subject inside and out, and I'm not going to trip on something I've missed."

Be skeptical. "Whenever I listen to somebody, whatever they're saying to me, my first step is to assume they mean exactly the opposite and I start there. I say to myself, 'Now what is it that will benefit them from what they just said to me?' I don't want to be cynical and untrusting, but I know that the human mind is capable of trickery and self-deception. It is human nature to try to cast oneself in the best possible light. It's helpful to keep this in mind.

"It's the old journalism cliché, 'If your mother says she loves you, check it out.' Unfortunately, I hate to say that it's worked pretty well."

You will get it wrong sometimes. "A certain percentage of the human race is going to hate you. There's no dishonor in being wrong, as long as you can figure it out, 'fess up, and move on."

Writing itself is just bricklaying, there's nothing glamorous about it. "It's practice, practice, practice. It does not get easier because I continually push myself to write a better sentence, and to be more attentive to everything about good writing. When I make a grammatical error, I die a little bit."

TV commentator v. writer: "They are very different skills. I find that I am braver in writing than I am on television. On TV, you're always aware there's somebody in your ear, there are a million things to worry about when you're on television, from your hair to 'am I holding my stomach in?' You want to be gracious on television, but I have no such hesitations in print. I am more myself when I write. TV makes you aware of other people and we all want to be liked. Writing doesn't care."

How to stand out among millions of opiners: "It is so hard to find your place in the world because everybody has an opinion and now everyone has his own little soapbox. All you've got over the other guy is your best stuff—and it needs to be better than his.

"The most important thing is to read. Read literature. I grew up without television, and the only exemption from physical labor in my household was reading. So I kept my nose in a book pretty much all my life growing up. I benefited from that enormously.

"Through reading you learn how to write. You learn other things of great value by becoming the kind of person who is thoughtful, and interesting and provocative, with the heart to say it.

"To stand out in the herd you have to say something. I don't mean being provocative for the sake of being provocative, or just for the sake of getting attention. Think hard and see what you have to say, and say it better.

"Most people are herding creatures and they will go with what's allowed in their particular neighborhood or peer group, seeking approval and acceptance. You have to shed yourself of those expectations and those needs.

"So read, think hard, and be brave. Be very brave."

From I Don't to I Do

By Kathleen Parker
January 30, 2013
Washington Post Writer's Group

More than perhaps anyone else in America, David Blankenhorn personifies the struggle so many have experienced over same-sex marriage.

First he was agnostic, then he was against it, now he's for it.

This is to say that Blankenhorn—a long-standing opponent of same-sex marriage—has shifted his energies to saving the institution of marriage, regardless of whom one chooses as a mate.

If you're unfamiliar with Blankenhorn, it is because he hasn't been barking his positions on television the way so many ideologues do. And this may be because he is not strictly an ideologue, but one of those rare people who agonize in search of the right thing.

As creator of the Institute for American Values, Blankenhorn initially sought to avoid the gay marriage issue altogether because it *was* so divisive—and because opposition necessarily meant hurting friends and often, family. Eventually, he wrote a book against same-sex marriage and testified against it as California's Proposition 8 was challenged in court.

Then, last summer he changed his mind.

Tuesday, Blankenhorn and more than 70 diverse signatories released a letter urging Americans to end the gay-marriage war and change the question from "Should gays marry?" to "How can we save marriage?"

Joining Blankenhorn are scholars, law professors, theologians and journalists, notably his former arch-rival Jonathan Rauch. Whether one is straight or gay, they say, the challenge is to figure out how to strengthen marriage for the broader benefit to society.

Blankenhorn's journey through the marriage minefield parallels that of many Americans who, though they held no animosity toward gays, weren't sure that changing the institution of marriage was in the best interest of society.

Like Blankenhorn, my greatest concern has been the effect on our nation's children. The operative questions, posed so well by traditional marriage warrior Maggie Gallagher, were: Do we want to codify the notion that one parent, either the mother or father, is dispensable? And, what effect might this have?

We have witnessed the fallout from broken families in the past several decades, during which divorce and out-of-wedlock births have skyrocketed. These trends have been wrought not by expanding the definition of marriage but by a general lowering of respect for the institution. Blankenhorn's group suggests that given Americans' evolving acceptance of same-sex marriage, we should refocus our energies on a goal that transcends sexual orientation.

His group's focus is on the disintegration of marriage in the middle and lower classes, which, they say, is creating a new underclass of inequality. As it happens, well-educated people tend to stay married in greater numbers, while the less educated—high school and no college—are becoming a subculture of economically depressed, single-parent families. Studies no longer need to be cited to convince us of what we know: Children from such homes have a lousy shot at the pursuit of happiness.

Blankenhorn still believes, as do most Americans, that a child benefits most from a loving mother and father committed in marriage. The United Nations Convention on the Rights of the Child even has designated this arrangement as a right. "Marriage," Blankenhorn has written, "is a gift that society bestows on its children."

But this gift has been badly damaged or, too often these days, withheld. Moreover, many same-sex couples today also have children. It is simply not possible to justify offering societal protections to only certain children. As Blankenhorn has recognized, it is in everyone's best interest that all children in all families have the security of parents committed through marriage with all its attendant rights and responsibilities.

In an op-ed last summer, Blankenhorn expanded on his vision:

"Once we accept gay marriage, might we also agree that marrying before having children is a vital cultural value that all of us should do more to embrace?" he asked. "Can we agree that, for all lovers who want their love to last, marriage is preferable to cohabitation?

"Can we discuss whether both gays and straight people should think twice before denying children born through artificial reproductive technology the right to know and be known by their biological parents?"

Now there's a feast for thought.

Blankenhorn's personal transformation has resulted in a welcome shift in the public debate. How clever of him to recognize that his allies in strengthening marriage are the very people who for so long have been excluded.

The sirens of the Pentagon

Kathleen Parker
January 28, 2013
Washington Post Writer's Group

It must be true what they say about women—that they are smarter, stronger, wiser and wilier than your average Joe.

How else could one explain the magical thinking that apparently has prompted Defense Secretary Leon Panetta and Gen. Martin Dempsey, chairman of the Joint Chiefs of Staff, to abandon all reason and lift the ban on women in direct combat?

Methinks the boys have been outmaneuvered.

This is a terrible idea for reasons too numerous to list in this space, which forces me to recommend my 2008 book, *Save the Males*, in which I devote a chapter to the issue. The most salient point happens to be a feminist argument: Women, because of their inferior physical capacities and greater vulnerabilities upon capture, have a diminished opportunity for survival.

More on this, but first let's be clear. Arguments against women in direct combat have nothing to do with courage, skill, patriotism or dedication. Most women are equal to most men in all these categories, and are superior to men in many other areas, as our educational graduation rates at every level indicate. Women also tend to excel as sharpshooters and pilots.

But ground combat is one area in which women, through quirks of biology and human nature, are not equal to men—a difference that should be celebrated rather than rationalized as incorrect.

Remember, we're not talking about female officers of a certain age pacing the hallways of the Pentagon when we speak of placing women in combat, though perhaps we should be. My favorite bumper sticker remains: "I'm out of estrogen and I have a gun."

We're potentially talking about 18-year-old girls, notwithstanding their "adult" designation under the law. (Parents know better.) At least 18-year-old males have the advantage of being gassed up on testosterone, the hormone that fuels not just sexual libido but, more to the point, aggression. To those suffering a sudden onset of the vapors, ignore hormones at your peril.

Now, hold the image of your 18-year-old daughter, neighbor, sister or girlfriend as you follow these facts, which somehow have been ignored in the advancement of a fallacy. The fallacy is that because men and women are equal under the law, they are equal in all endeavors and should have all access to the same opportunities. This is true except when the opportunity requires certain characteristics.

Fact: Females have only half the upper-body strength as males—no small point in the field.

Further to the fallacy is the operating assumption that military service is just another job. The rules of civil society do not apply to the military, which is a top-down organization in which the rules are created to maximize efficiency in killing enemies. It is not just another job that can be managed with the human resources department's Manual on Diversity and Sensitivity.

The argument that women's performance on de facto front lines in Iraq and Afghanistan has proved concerns about combat roles unwarranted is false logic. Just because women in forward support companies can return fire when necessary—or die—doesn't necessarily mean they are equal to men in combat.

Unbeknownst perhaps to many civilians, combat has a very specific meaning in the military. It has nothing to do with stepping on an IED or suffering the consequences of being in the wrong place at the wrong time. It means AGGRESSIVELY ENGAGING AND ATTACKING the enemy with deliberate offensive action, with a high probability of face-to-face contact.

If the enemy is all around you—and you need every available

person—that is one set of circumstances. To ask women to engage vicious men and risk capture under any other is beyond understanding. This is not a movie or a game. Every objective study has argued against women in direct combat for reasons that haven't changed.

The threat to unit cohesion should require no elaboration. But let's leave that obvious point to pedants and cross into enemy territory where somebody's 18-year-old daughter has been captured. No one wants to imagine a son in these circumstances either, obviously, but women face special tortures. And, no, the rape of men has never held comparable appeal.

We can train our men to ignore the screams of their female comrades, but is this the society we want to create? And though some female veterans of the Iraq and Afghanistan wars have endured remarkable suffering, their ability to withstand or survive violent circumstances is no rational argument for putting American girls and women in the hands of enemy men.

It will kill us in the end.

Suzette with Colin Powell

Suzette with David Halberstam

Suzette using a stepstool to address the NSNC in 2005 at the Texas conference

Journalist, author and *Time Magazine* columnist Hugh Sidey who covered the American presidency

Suzette with Maggie Thatcher

Suzette with Stormin' Norman Schwarzkopf

Suzette with Navajo painter R. C. Gorman

Suzette with author Scott Turow, who wrote *Presumed Innocent* and *Burden of Proof*

Suzette with then "Drug Czar" William J. Bennett, director of the office of the national drug control policy under George H. W. Bush

Suzette with *New York Times* and Pulitzer Prize winning columnist William L. Safire

Suzette holding a pencil at two years old, making her a writer since 1956!

"We have too many high-sounding words, and too few actions that correspond with them."
-Abigail Adams (1797-1801)

CONNIE SCHULTZ

Politics, Op-Ed and Everyday Folks

Columnist Connie Schultz, 55, is working-class proud and known for writing about the rights of women and laborers. She is impassioned by politics and she is willful.

In 1993, *The Cleveland Plain Dealer* hired Schultz as a reporter, and she became a columnist in 2002. Three years later, Schultz won the Pulitzer Prize, the second such honor for *The Plain Dealer* and its first in 50 years. Yet her winning columns had never appeared on the op-ed page.

From the start, she butted heads with management over her choice of topics for Arts and Life, an atypical section for her interests.

"I wrote about guns in my first three weeks, I wrote about Nazis, using the Confederate flag. There are so few women who get paid to do this, and I was not going to waste it. I feel so strongly that women need to have more voices in the national and the international debates of the day, and I was not going to waste my space by writing about pantyhose.

"My editor-in-chief would come down and I'd get a lecture, or my department supervisor would tear her hair out, but my attitude was, 'I'm a feminist, a liberal in Ohio, and you put me on the Arts and Life pages. You can't tell me you didn't know what you were getting. Just because you put me there, it doesn't mean I have to subscribe to old notions of what that column was going to look like.' It was a constant battle until the Pulitzer, and it really changed the dynamic in the newsroom for me."

Schultz's career in journalism began in fits and starts. She graduated in 1979 with a major in journalism from Kent State University and did volunteer writing for years. This mother of two turned 30 in 1987, and had a now-or-never insight.

"It was one of those crystallizing moments. I had been doing a little bit here and there, volunteering for the school newsletter, doing anything to just keep writing. I was very happy to be a mother, very happy to have these children in my life, but it was also painfully clear that it was not going to be enough for me personally. I needed to write, I yearned to write, and I loved reporting. I had a little chat with myself, essentially, that said, 'If you don't get started now, if you don't take this career seriously, it's never going to happen.'"

Schultz's first freelance column explored her annoyance at her son's school for only inviting men to coach the softball teams. "I grew up playing on boys and men's teams, and I knew how to play, and I knew how to coach. From there I started doing a lot of essays and then profiles, too."

Her independent pieces ran in a variety of publications, such as *The Plain Dealer Sunday Magazine*. "The Sunday magazine had run about 40 pieces by me before I was hired in December 1993."

While there she honed her reporting skills for 10 years. "For anyone who wants to become a columnist, you really should be a reporter first. It teaches you a set of skills that I don't know how you learn otherwise.

"You learn how to write well when you have to do stories that you don't want to do. No matter what the story is, I want my standard to be very high."

Her 2005 Pulitzer for her work at the *Plain Dealer* brought recognition and offers. In 2007, Creators Syndicate syndicated Schultz for op-ed, and that same year, she published a book, *Life Happens: And Other Unavoidable Truths.* In 2010 Schultz signed a contract with *Parade Magazine* to write personal essays, and wrote for all three venues until her departure from the *Plain Dealer* in 2011.

Schultz unfurled her blue-collar banner as a champion of the working class from the start of her newspaper career, a point of view that later may have tipped the scales in her favor for the Pulitzer Prize.

"My first column was about my dad's lunch pail because he vowed we'd never carry one. A reader kept a pair of his father's work boots with my column inside and he told me, 'They're in my office and I spend every day trying to fill those shoes.'

"You have conversations with people over the years, including some who sat on the Pulitzer board. I'm told that the column that stayed in their heads was the one about the tip jar in coat check, and how management was taking all the tips.

"Some of the saddest emails to me after I left *The Plain Dealer* were from readers who said, 'Who's going to fight for us now?' Coming from factory workers, and waitresses and hourly wage earners from Walmart, that kind of stuff really broke my heart because I'm still writing about it. I have more readers than I've ever had, but they're not seeing it because *The Plain Dealer* doesn't run my column."

Schultz married Congressman Sherrod Brown (Democrat, Ohio) and took a leave of absence from *The Plain Dealer* in 2006 to work on his U.S. Senate campaign. He won the election, and, when she returned to newspaper in 2007, folks speculated as to whether she could write open, in-depth opinions while married to a politician.

Her 2007 book, *And His Lovely Wife: A Campaign Memoir of the Woman Beside the Man*, chronicles experiences with her husband on his senate campaign trail. There are challenges and benefits to such a pairing, and she walks the fine line of public perception.

"I have a strong set of ethics and I'm very open about what I do. If I were any more transparent, I'd be Saran™ Wrap.

"I didn't set out to marry a member of Congress. I was a single mom for 10 years, and he'd been a single dad for 18 years. I love him very much, and he's a great husband. Sherrod says he wouldn't have won the Senate race without me, and I would not have won the Pulitzer without him. We make each other braver.

"The challenges are evident. I have to be very clear with myself and with my editors that I keep track of the lines. For example, I don't write about legislation that he is proposing. During the healthcare debate, Sherrod was prominent, so I had to restrain myself.

"I have access being married to him but I can't write about it. I have met powerful people who are comfortable with me, and that may irk some journalists."

Schultz will not be the last female journalist married to a politician. In fact, such relationships may become more common with time, and she predicted, "As more and more women forge their way in careers, more women will be marrying men with equally public lives."

Criticism has never stopped Schultz from telling true stories about what politics and corporate actions mean in terms of the prices paid by everyday folks. A striking element of her style is to move readers without manipulating their emotions.

"I certainly want people to feel something. I want them to think, and I want them to feel, but the more emotional the subject matter, the more matter-of-factly I try to lay out the facts of it because I don't want readers to feel manipulated. There are too many columnists who go toward melodrama. They work it too hard to make people feel something.

"An example that always comes to mind is when I wrote about a factory worker in Jackson, Ohio. He and his fellow workers were all union members and locked out by the company that was trying to break the union. It was the job he'd had for three decades. I talked to enough people, and they all described him the same way; the kind of guy who whistled gospel music on the factory floor, a happy man, a kindhearted man.

"It was one of the main businesses of that town, and, over the course of the next two years, he got worse and worse because he couldn't find decent work. I talked to his daughter at length, which is how I got so many details. Her father tried to work for Walmart, but finally he called his daughter and said, 'I can't do this. They want us to wear matching vests and sing these songs in the morning. I'm a man and I need to feel like a man.'

"He increasingly got worse. The daughter is college-educated, the first in the family. She's got her masters in nursing. Her mother calls her on Sunday morning and says, 'You better get over here right away, there's something wrong with Daddy.'

"She gets over there, and he's in a fetal position on the floor banging his head against the rug. They put him in the car, and, all the way to the emergency room, he's chanting, 'A man who cannot provide for his family is unworthy in the eyes of God.' He's rocking in the back seat saying this over and over again. He's in [the hospital] for about 24 hours, they bring him home, and he says he's going to go for a walk. It took more than 50 people and two days to find him. He shot himself in the head.

"I found out about this a year after it happened, and I asked his daughter, 'How are you doing now?'

"She added, 'I pray to God every night.'
"I responded, 'Do you mind if I ask what your prayer is?'
"She said, 'Well, a lot of nights, it's simply dear God, I'm broken.'
That was my walk-off and I basically told the story just like I told you. You don't get into a big thing about how awful this company was.

"It was obvious the company was awful. They moved the company to Mexico, so it was clear it was about getting out. They couldn't break the union, and they couldn't pay the workers less money, so they were just going to leave.

"It was important for me to tell that story. I worked very hard on that column, and I decided it really had to be one where you laid down the bones, you put a little flesh on them, but you don't pad. You let the readers feel what they are going to feel."

Connie Schultz's Writing Process, Tips, and Advice

Schultz's goal is to get readers talking. "I want to start a conversation. Maybe the conversation is just in their heads, or they bring it up to someone else, or it's on Facebook. Let's have a conversation. I seldom feel that I've said everything that needs to be said on any issue, so I want to start that conversation."

Stick to a schedule. "It really is about putting the seat of your pants into the seat of your chair. Right now I'm working on my first novel, and it requires the same thing: discipline, first and foremost. You can't do anything without discipline, and it's certainly true with writing. There are no excuses, and all they do is prevent you from getting better as a writer."

Set your own writing standards. Schultz said, "You will meet any number of editors who will disappoint you because their standards are not your standards. Then you will meet some who are all that good and can really help you improve, but no matter who you are reporting to, or whoever is getting your story, you have to have a standard that is very high."

Relate to readers in a personal way. "My editor, Stuart Warner, one of the best editors I ever had, once said, 'If you share personal information, and you write the occasional lighter column, people who disagree with everything you say politically are going to read you because they are just like you. They love their dog, they love their children, they are single parents just like you.' That was some of the best advice I ever got."

Write the way you speak. "I try to have a conversational approach when I write. I do not want to be an attempted 'Voice of God,' wagging her finger from the mountaintop and saying, 'You should think the way I do.' That's not helpful. I can't imagine building any bridges with that. There's too much of that writing out there. I always try to have a conversational tone.

"I read aloud my columns to make sure they would sound the way I talk. The highest praise from a reader is when they tell me, 'I feel like I'm having a conversation with you at my kitchen table.' That's what I want them to feel."

Vital issue? Stay the course. For a short time, many columnists become impassioned about a problem, gun possession, for example, and then they stop writing about it, they let go. In order to make a difference, a matter must stay alive in the public eye. Yet, Schultz understands why writers might be reluctant to continue pursuit of an issue, "We let get go, in part, because as columnists there's always a part of us that says, 'Oh, I don't want them [readers] to roll their eyes and say, 'Again?'"

But Schultz doesn't let go. Her approach is to "mix things up," such as writing columns that can be, at turns, hard hitting, personal, or humorous about a particular issue, such as gun control. The important thing is do not let a crucial issue fade from public consciousness.

"I don't want to be a one-hit wonder. One of the great things about being a columnist is that you can revisit issues time and again, and you can indicate when readers have changed your mind or made you think about things differently or more deeply. I really do want to start a conversation and build a relationship with readers."

At times veer away from your typical writing style. In 2012 when children were fatally shot in Newtown, Connecticut, Schultz took a column writing approach that was different from her typical storytelling style.

"I found the interview that Noah Pozner's mother gave to *The Jewish Daily Forward*. Noah Pozner was one of the little boys killed in Newton, and she actually described his body a bit. As a Jewish woman, it is very unusual to have an open casket now. She shared why she had it and why she wanted the governor to look at him. There was a cloth covering the bottom half of his face because it had been blown away. In one of his hands, she put an angel rock in it, the other hand she couldn't because it had been blown away. He was shot 11 times.

"As soon as I read that interview, I thought, 'I'm going to do something I normally don't do. I'm going to excerpt at length from that interview because there is no paraphrasing that.' It was so unusual in the wake of the Newtown shootings to hear anything of the physical evidence of destruction that happened."

Having a column in print is not important. There was a time when being located in a specific newspaper section dictated a columnist's topics, and the paper's circulation defined the size of a columnist's readership. Today, the Internet widens the possibilities.

"What's interesting to me is that now it almost doesn't matter where you start in the print edition of a paper because people are going to find you online. That has really changed the dynamic for columnists. We can explore more topics no matter where we are."

Do not write for free. Schultz has a longstanding rule: never write for free. The Internet has induced an insatiable appetite for content, yet many writers have difficulty finding paid venues. Consequently, many authors are willing to give away their work in exchange for visibility and promotion of their work.

However, since content providers are on the lookout for free workers, do not develop a reputation as one. "I wasn't going to write for any publication of note without getting paid for it. It's important to get your work out there, but if you keep doing it for free, everyone will know. If you value your work, editors will value it as well. Social media makes it easier to drive traffic to your work."

Promote others. Schultz often supports other writers by sharing their links with her 120,000 Facebook subscribers, "Male bloggers get hired more often to be columnists. I don't envy young women writers who are trying to sort this out. When I post a link to a story, I get thanks from reporters because it drives traffic to their pieces. I would fail at my profession if I only promoted my work. Especially as a woman, I feel such an obligation to promote the work of other women."

A good reputation will overcome reluctant sources. Over the years, Schultz has developed the following strategies to encourage the hesitant to come forward with information.

"I've reached that point in my career, I don't have a lot of people not willing to talk to me. They've figured out it's not a good idea to not respond. With every story you do, you are building a reputation for yourself. Every interview contributes to that.

"Interview others first. Then set up interview with the institution. I tell them I'm going to write about it anyway.

"Do all the other reporting first. You track down all the facts, get a body of evidence, and then lower the boom.

"Be tough but fair. If you make the tough calls or have the tough conversations, people will respect you. Traditional journalism has it over bloggers that way.

"You have to report. Reporting informs your opinion or recalibrates it."

Stress will not produce creativity. "It's important to relax. When you write columns and you're trying to figure out a topic, or when you're trying to find out what to say, I've learned to give myself a little bit of time for that to happen. You do gain a certain level calm and confidence with time. The column will come, and you have to get out of your own way sometimes.

"If it's 2:00 p.m., and I don't have to file until five, then I throw a load of clothes in the wash. I take my dog Franklin, and we go for a 45-minute walk. I have a little notebook in my pocket in case something comes to mind, and by the time I get back, I feel more awake, and ready to finish up my column. Boom! It just slides off the fingers. Sometimes you have to walk away for a little bit and then come back.

"That only comes with experience. It doesn't mean there aren't times when I think, 'Oh my God, I have only half an hour left and I still haven't figured out my walk-off!' But I've learned to give myself that mental space. I don't panic if I go to bed the night before and I'm not sure what I'm going to write about yet.

"It does come, and nothing gets in my way faster than panic."

Improving the lives of others through one's writing can become a legacy that lasts well beyond a writer's lifespan. Notoriety itself is short lived. Schultz said, "If the only legacy is my own success, then it dies with me. Too many columnists get caught up in self-importance. It's about the work and how much we want to invest in investigation and thinking things through.

"We can have a real effect on people's lives, and we have to take that responsibility seriously."

A Promise in a Lunch Pail

By Connie Schultz
October 2002
The Plain Dealer

I want Dad's lunch pail.

I imagine it on my desk, right next to my computer, holding all my pens, notebooks and stick-'em pads. A reminder of a promise made, and a promise kept.

So I pester him. "Have you found it yet?"

"I don't even know if I have it anymore," he told me. "I may have thrown it out when I left the plant."

Please, no.

My father does not understand why his lunch pail matters to me, probably because he never thought his job mattered, either.

For 36 years, my dad worked in maintenance for the Cleveland Electric Illuminating Company. He was 20, already married and the father of two-month-old me when he walked through the doors of the power plant carrying a union card and a brand-new black metal lunch pail. He never replaced it. By the time he retired, there were holes on the bottom corners where metal nubs used to be.

That lunch pail is my most enduring childhood memory of life with Dad, who was big and burly and not much for small talk or late-night tucks into bed. Most evenings, it lay open on the kitchen counter until my mother filled the Thermos with milk and made four sandwiches wrapped in wax paper. Sometimes she drew a funny picture on his paper napkin, or scribbled a little note.

"I love you," she would write in her loopy backhand. "Meatloaf for dinner!"

When I was little, I didn't understand what Dad did for a living. His job was simply the thing that kept him away. He worked a lot of overtime, and even when he came home on time, he had little to say about his day. Little good, anyway.

"You could teach a monkey to do what I do," he said some evenings to no one in particular, staring straight ahead as he nursed his Stroh's. At 6-foot-1, 220 pounds, my father was a giant to me, and I could not bear to imagine him any other way. I would scurry off, unwilling to meet his gaze.

Once I started working for a living, I occasionally prodded my father to tell me about his work.

I wanted the reality check, the reminder that no matter how hard I thought I was working, I would never come close to the hard labor he knew.

"What did you do there?" I would ask. "Tell me about the equipment you used. Who did you talk to all day long?"

He was never interested in the conversation. "It was a job," he'd say. "Not a career."

That's probably why he can't understand why I want his lunch pail, but he's promised to keep looking for it. To Dad, it is a reminder of the job he hated. To me, it is an enduring symbol of the promise he made to his four young children.

"You kids are never going to carry one of these to work," he'd tell us, over and over.

"You kids are going to college.

He made good on his promise. I am the oldest, so I was the first to go. Whenever I came home for a weekend, my dad would take me with him to run errands and, inevitably, we'd end up at one of his favorite taverns. His buddies always said the same thing when we walked through the door. Here comes the college kid.

Dad would beam. "Yup, she's never going to carry a lunch pail, by God." A dozen glasses would rise in the air.

My story is as old as the bricks under Cleveland's earliest streets. I am the child of working-class parents determined they would be the last of their kind. And there was the same unspoken deal in thousands of households. We'll send you kids away, but don't you ever forget where you came from.

As if we could.

I went to college, and so the heaviest piece of equipment I have to lift is a laptop. I became a writer. That is what I do.

My home is now in a neighborhood where the railroad tracks groan under the weight of the commuter train, instead of the freight trains of my childhood. That is where I live.

But I am also the girl whose father carried a lunch pail for 36 years.

And that is who I am.

Here's a little tip about gratuities

By Connie Schultz
April 1, 2004
The Plain Dealer

If you've ever used a coat check, you probably noticed a tip jar on the counter at evening's end.

You might stick a bill or two into that jar without even thinking about who is getting the tip. You probably assume the person behind the counter, usually a woman, is getting the money.

That's certainly what I always assumed. From now on, I'm going to ask.

In the last year, I have attended three charity events at Windows on the River, a banquet hall at the Powerhouse in the Flats. At the end of each dinner, I picked up my wrap at the coat-check counter.

One of those times, I pointed to the large tip jar bulging with bills and said to the weary clerk, "Well, at least you get a decent amount of tips for standing here."

She shook her head and said, "Oh, we don't get to keep those."

I thought I misheard her. "What?"

"We don't keep the tips."

"Who does?" I asked.

"Management."

When I asked her how that made her feel, she sighed. "They say they use it to give us a Christmas party."

Nowhere was there a sign indicating that the pile of bills in the tip jar was going, not to the clerk, but to management.

Recently, I attended another dinner at Windows on the River. This time, the tips were stuffed into a large, opaque box. I watched as one person after another shoved bills into the slot on the top.

"Who gets these tips?" I asked the coat-check clerk.

She resisted telling me, but I pressed. "Management," she said softly.

"How does that make you feel?" I asked. She shrugged her shoulders. "Life isn't fair, right?"

This week, I called Kristine Jones, the general manager for Windows.

"Why are you asking about this?" she said. "Why do you care?"

The "girls," she insisted, are happy with the current arrangement. "It's not like they're standing there all night. The girls check the coats and then wait on tables until the last hour. And they're already paid an hourly wage."

Later that same day, two vice presidents—Dave Grunenwald and Pat McKinley—called on speakerphone from Jacobs International Management Co., which owns Windows.

"We're confused," Grunenwald said. "This is newsworthy?"

They were brimming with assurances. Their 30 or so employees— some of the kindest, most professional servers I've ever encountered—are paid more than the minimum wage.

How much more, they wouldn't say. The company matches any 401(k) contribution they can make but offers no health insurance because they're all part time.

And they get a free meal. "Some places charge their employees for food," McKinley said.

Grunenwald and McKinley say they collect only $800 a year in that tip jar. Hard to believe, judging from the amount stuffed into the box last Friday night. "We match it for their Christmas party," Grunenwald said.

When I asked if they'd ever let the employees decide between keeping the tips and having a party, they fell silent.

That would be a "no."

"Why does this matter?" they asked.

Dignity is non-negotiable, writes scholar Vartan Gregorian. It is also every human's birthright, and management's blatant rankism at Windows is an assault on the dignity of all involved.

Generous patrons are misled. Hard-working employees must stand silently by as they watch management walk off with hundreds, perhaps thousands, of dollars intended for them.

"Maybe we need to rethink this," Grunenwald said. "Maybe we do," echoed McKinley.

There's no maybe about it. Both union and industry officials say keeping the coat-check tips is unacceptable.

General manager Jones was unrepentant. "I don't ever think about who's getting the tip when I use a coat check," she said. "I don't care."

Then she added, "I don't think anyone else cares who gets the tip, either."

I think she's wrong.

What do you think?

"Hell begins the day that God grants you the vision to see all that you could have done, should have done, and would have done, but did not do."
-Goethe

JEFFREY L. SEGLIN

Ethics as Op-Ed

Each week in newspapers throughout the U.S. and Canada, Jeffrey L. Seglin resolves ethical dilemmas posed by readers in his op-ed column, *The Right Thing*, which is syndicated by Tribune Media Services.

Helping readers through conflicts does make general ethics a perfect fit for the op-ed page. "When you look at the work that Ellen Goodman did for *The Globe*, she wrote all the time about tough decisions that people make about inequities in the world. It's just that mine happens to be more pronounced or more defined," Seglin said.

Applied ethics, an examination from a moral standpoint of issues arising in personal and public life, is how Seglin describes his work. However, one perfect answer to any dilemma is not what he provides. Notions of right and wrong are obvious to most people, but the main challenge is to address areas of gray. His task is to offer the best resolution from multiple choices based on the needs of the person writing to him.

Jeff explained, "You have philosophers and theologians who wrote about ethics, and there are rules-based people who say the rules have to apply to everyone or it's not ethical. Then there are utilitarian people who say that it's OK to bend the rules as long as the greatest good is for the greatest number of people.

"When there are huge disagreements, it's not always because someone's right or someone's wrong. It's that people come at making decisions from different viewpoints.

"It's the approach to the problem as opposed to the viewpoint itself that is at the root of conflicts. People never take the time to ask, 'How did you come up with that?'"

Many a columnist discovers his niche by chance like Seglin, who did his graduate work at Harvard Divinity School, studying literature and theology, but never expected to write about ethics. "I took ethics courses, but it wasn't my specialty."

It really began by writing about bad business decisions. From 1989 to 1998, Seglin was an editor and writer for *Inc. Magazine*, a publication for small businesses, where he wrote a technology column, book reviews and reported on a variety of subjects.

When articles about unethical business practices drew significant mail from readers, Seglin took note and acted on it. "We decided we'd do a series of short features on people who made decisions that could be perceived as unethical choices."

In 1998 Seglin decided to leave *Inc Magazine* for a fellowship at the Center for the Study of Values in Public Life at Harvard. "I wanted to work on a book on ethics built from the stories I had written."

As he was leaving the magazine, Seglin received a phone call. *The New York Times* was redoing its Sunday business pages, and Seglin was asked for a reference on a writer whom *The Times* wanted to hire. During their conversation, the editor shared with Seglin the candidates's reluctance to relocate from Washington, D.C. to New York, and admitted the odds were against the hire.

"Realizing that he wasn't going to get him, he asked me, 'Well, what do you do?' I told him I was about to do a fellowship on business ethics, and he said, 'Well, we're revising that section. Would you be interested in writing a business ethics column as a prototype?' and that's how it got started."

In 1998, during his fellowship, Seglin authored *The Good, the Bad, and Your Business: Choosing Right When Ethical Dilemmas Pull You Apart*, which was published by Wiley Press in 2000. That same year Seglin also started a monthly business ethics column for *The New York Times* and he said, "It had a very odd sequence. It ran every third Sunday, so it terms of building traction, that's very hard to do. Readers don't look for something that runs every third Sunday."

However, in the days before email and online posting readers mailed letters of feedback on his column. By 2004, *The Right Thing* changed its focus from business ethics to general ethics, and became a syndicated weekly by The New York Times Syndicate. It was acquired by Tribune Media Services in 2010 and continues to be syndicated throughout the U.S. and Canada.

Jeffrey L. Seglin's Writing Process, Insights, and Advice

In addition to his work as a journalist and author, Seglin is the Director of the Communications Program at the John F. Kennedy School of Government at Harvard where he lectures on public policy and teaches opinion writing. Separately in this book, Seglin shares advice from his course in op-ed writing. Below are insights into his personal process.

No snap judgments: Resolving a reader's ethical dilemma is not a matter of instinct or a gut reaction. "That spells trouble," he said. Yet a decision that is not a bad choice *per se* also does not make it the best choice. Help a reader recognize there may be other options. Surprisingly, few people consider the following questions:

Does your decision conflict with local laws?

What are the ramifications of your choice?

What are the possible unintended consequences?

Does the decision work toward the wholeness and health of the group involved?

What approach is best for the individuals seeking guidance, given their background and personal beliefs?

A Simpler Way, a book written by Margaret Wheatley and Myron Kellner-Rogers, proves helpful and Seglin shared a book excerpt:

"Ethics is how we behave when we decide we belong together. Daily we see this interplay of ethics and belonging in our own lives. We want to be part of an organization. We observe what is accepted or rewarded and we adapt. But these ethics are not always good. We may agree to behaviors that go against personal or societal values. Months or years later, we dislike the person we have become. Did we sacrifice some essential aspect of ourselves in order to stay with an organization? What was the price of belonging?"

Engage the reader with variety. "You're trying to keep it fresh and it's tough to do it every week. It's a challenge, so I try to mix it up with questions from my readers, my personal anecdotal stuff, or something from the news. Occasionally, I look for reactions to a column, and I'll try to build a column around the reactions, particularly if someone tells me how wrong I was. If enough people tell me how wrong I was, I try to revisit it, but generally, I avoid repetition of a topic."

When possible, keep it personal. What gets readers riled up still surprises him. They are never big issues like taxes, and he joked, "The kind of things that people really seem to get worked up about are things that are closer to home like why is my neighbor stealing my garbage?"

Over the years, Seglin observes reader response is most high when private matters are involved. "I try to make sure that I focus on the more deeply personal for readers, whether it is a business setting or a family setting."

Three questions vital to opinion writing: When Seglin teaches at Harvard Kennedy School, he believes the answers to the following three questions are essential to writing an opinion:

Do I have a point?

What is it?

Who cares?

He said, "It's the last of those that's really important. If you have a point and it's a really clear point, and there's an audience who cares, then I think that there's a possibility of being a success."

Take advantage of unique access. Focus on being at the right place at the right time and then make the most of it. Seglin recalled how one of his graduate students emailed him the night before class asking permission to be late. The young man had a chance to attend the return to Harvard's campus of the first ROTC class since it was banned in the 1970's. The student managed an invitation although he was one of the few people attending who was not a ROTC member. His aim was to use his unique access to write an op-ed piece, which later ran in *The Wall Street Journal*.

"I tell my students to focus on being curious, on doing diligent research, putting yourself in the right place at the right time, and having a unique take on something, but it also has to have three things: Do you have a point? What is it? Who cares? And he had all three."

Is the specificity of ethics a marketing advantage? "You would think it would make me attractive because there are so many unethical folks out there, but I'm not sure."

The Right Thing appears on op-ed pages but also has run in the lifestyle, advice, and religion sections of newspapers. While the subject of ethics has breadth, Seglin wonders if it works against him. "I sometimes don't know if people know where to find me. It's carried wherever the editor wants to carry it, which is both the beauty and challenge of being syndicated. I don't have a lot of say over where the papers run it."

Take a strong stand. When Seglin's column first ran in *The New York Times*, the Sunday editor allowed him to write in a way whereby readers drew their own conclusions. Later, however, the syndicate editors pushed him to take a clear position on right and wrong and even added the ending line to his column: "The right thing to do is…"

Initially, Seglin was reluctant to make such pronouncements, but eventually agreed that clarity is empowering to readers.

A second opinion strengthens a draft. Find someone whose critique you trust. For example, his wife, Nancy, was his first book editor, and she casts a discerning eye on all his work. "In terms of sorting things out, she'll ask me 'How did you get from here to here?' It's helpful for me to have another set of eyes before I submit it to my editor."

A fascination with complexity pulled Seglin into the orbit of general ethics, an attraction that has sustained him throughout his career. "I love trying to figure out how people make decisions. I just love it in my professional life, I love thinking about the people I write about. I love thinking about it when I'm working with students in my full-time work, and thinking about it as a parent. I just get great joy in trying to figure out how people make the choices they make."

Jeffrey L. Seglin's column, The Right Thing, *is syndicated weekly throughout the U.S. and Canada. He is the Director of the Communications Program at the John F. Kennedy School of Government at Harvard where he lectures on public policy and teaches opinion writing. He created the following material, which he graciously has given permission to use.*

An op-ed piece derives its name from originally having appeared opposite the editorial page in a newspaper. Today, the term is used more widely to represent a column that represents the strong, informed, and focused opinion of the writer on an issue of relevance to a targeted audience.

Distinguishing Characteristics of an Op-Ed or Column
Partly, a column is defined by where it appears, but it shares some common characteristics:
•	Typically, it is short, between 750 and 800 words.
•	It has a clearly defined point.
•	It has a clearly defined point of view.
•	It represents clarity of thinking.
•	It contains the strong, unique voice of the writer.

Questions to Ask Yourself When Writing an Op-Ed or Column
•	Do I have a clear point to make?
•	What is it?
•	Who cares? (Writing with a particular audience in mind can inform how you execute your column. Who is it that you are trying to convince? Why are you targeting that specific reader?)
•	Is there substance to my argument?

Topic and Theme
Every successful op-ed piece or column must have a clearly defined topic and theme.
•	Topic: the person, place, issue, incident or thing that is the primary focus of the column. The topic is usually stated in the first paragraph.
•	Theme: another level of meaning to the topic. What's the big, overarching idea of the column? What's your point? Why is your

point important? The theme may appear early in the piece or it may appear later when it may also serve as a turning point into a deeper level of argument.

Research

While columns and op-ed pieces allow writers to include their own voice and express an opinion, to be successful the columns must be grounded in solid research. Research involves acquiring facts, quotations, citations or data from sources and personal observation. Research also allows a reader to include sensory data (touch, taste, smell, sound, or sight) into a column. There are two basic methods of research:

•   Field research: going to the scene, interviews, legwork; primary materials, observations and knowledge
•   Library, academic or Internet research: using secondary materials, including graphs, charts and scholarly articles

Openings

The first line of an op-ed is crucial. The opening "hook" may grab the reader's attention with a strong claim, a surprising fact, a metaphor, a mystery or a counter-intuitive observation that entices the reader into reading more. The opening also briefly lays the foundation for your argument.

Endings

Every good column or op-ed piece needs a strong ending which has some basic requirements. It:
•   Echoes or answers introduction
•   Has been foreshadowed by preceding thematic statements
•   Is the last and often most memorable detail
•   Contains a final epiphany or calls the reader to action
There are two basic types of endings. An "open ending" suggests rather than states a conclusion, while a "closed ending" states rather than suggests a conclusion. The closed ending in which the point of the piece is resolved is by far the most commonly used.

Voice

Having a strong voice is critical to a successful column or op-ed piece. Columns are most typically conversational in tone, so you can imagine yourself have a conversation with your reader as you write (a short, focused conversation). But the range of voice used in columns can be wide: contemplative, conversational, descriptive, experienced, informative, informed, introspective, observant, plaintive, reportorial, self-effacing, sophisticated, humorous, among many other possibilities.

Sometimes what voice you use is driven by the publication for which you are writing. A good method of perfecting your voice is to get in the habit of reading your column or op-ed out loud. Doing so gives you a clear sense of how your piece might sound – what your voice may come off as – to your intended reader.

Revision Checklist
Some things to remember as you revise your op-ed or column before you submit it for publication:
•   Check clarity.
•   Check coherence and unity.
•   Check simplicity.
•   Check voice and tone. (Most are conversational; some require an authoritative voice.)
•   Check direct quotations and paraphrasing for accuracy.
•   Check to make sure you properly credit all sources though formal citations are not necessary.)
•   Check the consistency of your opinion throughout your op-ed or column.

Resources
Below are links to some online resources related to op-ed and column writing:

The Op-Ed Project (www.theopedproject.org) is a terrific resource for anyone looking to strengthen their op-ed writing. It provides tips on op-ed writing, suggestions about basic op-ed structure, guidelines on how to pitch op-ed pieces to publications, and information about top outlets that publish op-eds. Started as an effort to increase the number of women op-ed writers, The Op-Ed Project also regularly runs daylong seminars around the country.

"How to Write an Op-Ed Article" (www.newsoffice.duke.edu/duke_resources/oped), which was prepared by David Jarmul, Duke's associate vice president for news and communications, provides great guidelines on how to write a successful op-ed.

"How to Write Op-Ed Columns" (www.earth.columbia.edu/sitefiles/file/pressroom/media_outreach/OpEdGuide.doc), which was prepared by The Earth Institute at Columbia University, is another useful guide to writing op-eds. It contains a useful list of op-ed guidelines for top-circulation newspapers in the U.S.

"And Now a Word from Op-Ed" (www.nytimes.com/2004/02/01/opinion/01SHIP.html?pagewanted=all) offers some advice on how to think about and write op-eds from the Op-Ed editor of *The New York Times.*

The Harvard Kennedy School Communications Program regularly runs workshops on writing op-eds and columns as well as classes focusing on the topic. You can find out more about these by checking the HKS Communications Program's website (www.hkscommunicationsprogram.org)

Breaking the rules and winning a fan

By Jeffrey L. Seglin
April 5, 2011
Tribune Media Services

Is it ever OK to break the rules?

Late in March, my two grandsons lost their other grandfather, who died suddenly and unexpectedly. The death was a blow to the family and the loss of a lovely man.

Before my son-in-law told his two sons about his father's death, he called to ask if I would attend an autograph signing not far from my home in Boston that my oldest grandson was to attend the night of the wake in Chicago. My son-in-law wanted to be able to tell Evan that I would go to the event for which he had saved his money for months.

The rules of the autograph event were that you had to pay a separate fee for every item you wanted autographed. Evan had purchased an official NHL puck so he could have it signed by Boston Bruins center Patrice Bergeron.

I, of course, agreed to go, as did my wife.

The morning of the event, Evan called from Chicago. He asked me if he thought it would be OK to call me on my cell phone from the funeral home when I was scheduled to get the autograph.

"Maybe Patrice Bergeron will say hello to me," Evan said.

I reminded Evan that 500 tickets had been sold for the two-hour event, so we were likely to be rushed through. But I told him that I would try.

Being no hockey fan, I had no idea who Bergeron was. After Evan's call, I figured I should find out. In addition to playing for the Bruins, he had won a gold medal on the Canadian Olympic team. And buried in a sports reporter's blog was a reference to the fact that he had missed a game early in March because of his grandmother's death.

I called my son-in-law to tell him of the coincidence in Bergeron and Evan each losing a grandparent recently.

Figuring the phone call between Evan and Bergeron wouldn't happen, I printed up a sign that said, "Hello, Evan" as well as Bergeron's name and jersey number. (It's 37. I looked it up.) I figured my wife might hold the sign next to Bergeron when he was signing Evan's puck and we could snap a photo.

I also wrote to the owner of the shop where Bergeron was appearing explaining my grandson's loss and seeing if there was any possibility Bergeron would get on the phone with Evan. Terry Fox, co-owner of P&T Sports Cards, called me back, told me how moved she was, but that it was unlikely there would be time for a call. Still, she said she'd print out the email and give it to Bergeron's agent.

As expected, the event was packed. When we were third in line to get the autograph, Evan called. Someone grabbed the puck, ushered us up the line and, as Bergeron was signing it, I started to ask if he might talk to Evan. Without hesitation, he asked for the phone. He had seen the printout of the email and knew the story.

"I'm sorry for your loss," Bergeron said. "Hang in there." My wife's eyes welled up. And then Bergeron's eyes welled up too as he continued to talk. His agent put the sign I had made in front of Bergeron and asked him to "sign it for the kid." He did that too, breaking the rule about having to pay separately for each item signed.

Evan called later to thank me.

"What did you say when he told you he was sorry for your loss?" I asked.

"I told him I was sorry for his loss, too," Evan said.

Did Bergeron do the right thing by breaking the rules to sign an extra autograph? I'm biased, of course, but I like to think he did. I also know that he has new fans for life.

Sign of Our Times

By Jeffrey L. Seglin
April 30, 2013
Tribune Media Services

It's been an eventful few weeks in Boston.

The Boston Marathon, typically a celebratory event, was met with terror and tragedy. Just days later, people in the city and surrounding municipalities were voluntarily "sheltering in place" as law enforcement worked to find the men suspected of placing and detonating the bombs that killed and maimed.

Soon after the identities of the three people killed by the bomb blast were made known, photos of Martin Richard, the young boy from my part of Boston who died in one of the blasts, were shown with him holding a sign with the words, "No more hurting people" and "Peace."

An artist who runs a children's arts program in our community came up with the idea to have neighborhood children work on a banner featuring Martin's words. The plan was to paint the 85-foot banner on recycled acrylic wallpaper and then hang it from a bridge overlooking a highway that leads into Boston. Hundreds of kids showed up to paint on the Saturday after police caught the suspect. Adults showed up to help.

Early on Sunday morning, the artist emailed me to ask if she could give me a call. She told me she was concerned because she had not obtained a permit from the city of Boston to hang the banner. I reassured her that it was unlikely anyone would question the spirit of the banner or request that it be taken down for lack of a permit, but I suggested she call our district city councilor.

To ask him to secure a permit for us? she asked.

No, I responded, to ask him to come help us.

I figured that if our city councilor were involved in hanging the sign, the chances of the city taking it down were less likely.

Given that we still had no permit to hang the sign, was this the right thing to do?

If we had been asked to take the sign down, I certainly would have assisted in doing so (we didn't actually know if we needed a permit, although Boston being Boston, we assumed we did), but in this case, it seemed wise to heed the advice I first heard spoken years ago by Adm. Grace Hopper: "It's easier to ask forgiveness than it is to get permission."

As our artist friend stayed and painted with the children, a 12-year-old boy from the neighborhood, our city councilor and my wife and I walked up to the bridge to start attaching the unwieldy banner. As we struggled to keep it in place by attaching it to the bridge by using zip ties, other neighbors began stopping to help hold it in place. Soon, there were more than a couple dozen people attaching the sign.

Photos of the effort, including our city councilor affixing the banner to the bridge, were posted to Facebook. People shared images of the sign itself more than 3,800 times, often with messages of appreciation after having seen it while driving into the city.

No one asked where the permit was to hang the banner. No one asked that it be taken down. The response was just appreciation from people for seeing the words from a little boy asking people to do the right thing.

"Faith is being sure of what we hope for, and certain of what we do not see."
- Hebrews 11:1

CAL THOMAS

Op-Ed As Informed By Faith

Cal Thomas is the nation's most widely syndicated political columnist, appearing in 550 newspapers through Tribune Media Service. His commentaries are carried on 300 radio stations, and he is a contributor to the Fox News Channel. His work is branded as conservative and Thomas chafes against the term, "I don't like labels because it tends to let people define you according to their definition of the label. To some, conservative means you don't like women or that you hate black people."

Thomas was born in Washington, D.C. in 1942, graduated from American University, and at age 69, has been writing op-ed since 1984. Evangelical Christianity shapes his outlook and his opinions, but his topics are not limited to religious issues. "I try to be cutting edge. I wrote this piece about the Chicago school strike, and there's no religion in it, it's purely economics, kids trapped in failing schools. I have an integrated life, and faith is a normal part of my life."

Thomas asserts that the teachings of Jesus Christ underpin his worldview of everyday life and fuel his passion for writing op-ed. "I feel I have a purpose and a cause. God gave me my gift, and I promised him I would honor him if he allowed me this opportunity. I use this as a means of access to the hearts of my colleagues. I want to tell them that God loves them and has a plan for their lives."

When Thomas first pursued a columnist's byline in 1984, commentary informed by faith was absent from the op-ed pages. He sought to fill that niche. "I'm a follower of Jesus of Nazareth and I take seriously the word of God. I speak the kind of language and share the thought processes of millions of Americans who go to church, pay their taxes and are proud of this country."

During the 1960s and 1970s, Thomas was a reporter for the local NBC station in Washington, appearing on network radio and television. This position led to an active lecture schedule around the country.

One day, an idea sparked while he was speaking on stage. Sharing with attendees his desire to write a newspaper column, Thomas asked, "How many of you would subscribe to your paper if I were in it?" Every hand went up.

Buoyed by that experience, Thomas visited editors and persuaded newspapers that his column would increase readership. He asked, "How would you like hundreds of new subscribers?" It was a publisher's siren song, and in 1984 he began writing political op-ed from a moral perspective.

At the same time, he encouraged attendees at his lectures to support his column, "Call them and tell them I'm the reason you're subscribing." More often than not, it worked.

In 1987, syndication first came through Tom Johnson (best known today as the former president and CEO of CNN), and Thomas' work was later sold to Tribune Media Services. Like a professional athlete, Thomas was acquired, and now played for the new owners. "I'm not the only Christian writer, but I'm one of the very few who is writing an op-ed column, and it brings a certain value to the papers that carry me."

Thomas believes spiritual truths resonate with millions of readers. However, quoting Bible verses verbatim is not an effective way to write, and Thomas said, "God's principles work whether you acknowledge their source or not. If religious themes are part of the story, then I focus on that and try to explain it to my readers. I will frequently take a Biblical truth and paraphrase or adapt it to make my point, without saying that it is from scripture. It's more likely to be digested rather than my saying, 'Matthew said' in chapter and verse, although I do that when it is a relevant quote from the world's best-selling book."

Thomas has witnessed changes within the industry over decades that give him pause.

"I started in this business at 16, now I'm 69. It would have been nice to know that the newspaper industry was going to be in trouble. The newspaper industry committed suicide for not innovating or creating a pay wall for its subscribers. Once you give it away, you can't go back."

However, Thomas knows the industry's story is far from a conclusion, "I think we are in a great transition, but unlike the transition from agrarian America to the Industrial Revolution, we don't know what is yet to come."

Even as print journalism sorts out issues of a paying future, Thomas believes young journalists today have greater advantages compared to his early days. The Internet offers unlimited opportunity for individual platforms in reporting and column writing. Online research tools allow unprecedented access to information. A writer can tackle a unique story angle and find supporting facts or background easily. There is no excuse for inaccurate, lazy, or lackluster writing.

Thomas laughs when he recalls how he researched a story or a column in 1984, "I would have to leave my house, go to the library, and go through microfiche or books. I'd have to drive to the Press Club in Washington to read a foreign newspaper!"

Instant global access has overcome the past problem of censorship. Some newspaper editors would not run his columns, labeling Thomas's columns as too right wing. Now he simply posts all his work on his own website (www.calthomas.com) and his following has only increased.

Cal Thomas' Writing Process, Insights, and Advice

Sometimes Thomas will bang out a column in 10 minutes, but then there are days when he will be at his keyboard for three hours. He is not exactly sure what components are responsible for his longtime success. "It's just a gift. I didn't go through the gift line and decided what to pick and choose."

Read. "To be a good writer, you have to be a good reader. I read half a dozen newspapers a day, and then I'm on the Internet reading overseas newspapers."

Write simple sentences. "I write mostly in 'broadcast style,' no long sentences, no compound sentences. People can more easily absorb sound bites. The purpose is to be read by the community. If you use big words to show you are smarter than most, then people who are not smarter will not read you."

Stats are boring. "Statistics are helpful, but use too many and eyes will glaze over. Use them occasionally to bolster your argument."

No clichés. "A young person will be tempted to use clichés because you are new to writing. Your vocabulary may not be mature. I'd recommend reading the following books: *The Elements of Style* by William Strunk, Jr. and E.B. White, *Strictly Speaking* by Edwin Newman, *A Civil Tongue* by Edwin Newman, and *The Right Word in the Right Place at the Right Time: Wit and Wisdom from the Popular Language Column in the New York Times Magazine* by William Safire.

"Passion is good but it should not overcome a proper assessment of your abilities. English is such a beautiful language but so few people speak and write it well."

Have a purpose. "I'm trying to attract people to God. Maybe readers will ask, 'Why does he have this perspective?' I'm not explicit up front, but that's where I go to eventually."

Believe. "You want to convince people that your view is the correct one, or why write? Say what's on your mind, and let it come from the depths of your core beliefs. You have to feel it deep within your gut and soul with passion. Communicate with conviction."

To become a solid op-ed writer, the advantage is with those professionals who have served as news reporters. Thomas likened being a reporter to taking preliminary courses before advanced training in college. "When you're a reporter, you get out and you see stuff. You have to be out there to have more credibility and authority in what you're saying. When I was 20-something I thought I was ready to conquer the world, but I wasn't. Your experiences change you and your worldview. You can't microwave a career or a life."

My brother's valuable life

By Cal Thomas
May 5, 2012
Tribune Media Services

How does one measure whether a life was a success, or a failure?

Some would measure it by recognition, that is, how many knew the person's name. For others, the measure of a successful life would be the amount of wealth accumulated, or possessions held. Still others would say a life was successful if the person made a major contribution to society—in medicine, sports, politics, or the arts.

By that standard my brother, Marshall Stephen Thomas, who died January 5, was a failure. If, however, your standard for a successful life is how that life positively touched others, then my brother's life was a resounding success.

Shortly after he was born in 1950, Marshall was diagnosed with Down syndrome. Some in the medical community referred to the intellectually disabled as "retarded" back then, long before the word became a common schoolyard epithet. His doctors told our parents he would never amount to anything and advised them to place him in an institution. Back then, this was advice too often taken by parents who were so embarrassed about having a disabled child that they often refused to take them out in public.

Our parents wanted none of that. In the 50s, many institutions were snake pits where inhumanities were often tolerated and people were warehoused until they died, often in deplorable conditions. While they weren't wealthy, they were committed to seeing that Marshall had the best possible care, no matter how long he lived. Because of their dedication and thanks to the Kennedy family and their commitment to the rights, causes and issues related to the mentally and physically challenged, Marshall had a longer and better quality of life than might have been expected. He outlived his life expectancy by nearly 40 years. He lived his life dancing and singing and listening to music he loved.

Yes, it cost our parents a lot of money to give him the care they believed he deserved. They might have taken more vacations, owned a fancier house and driven a luxurious car, but before we valued things more than people, they valued Marshall more than any tangible thing. And that care rubbed off on me and other family members.

The stereotype about people who call themselves conservatives is that we don't care for the less fortunate. Even if that were true (which it isn't), Marshall deepened my sensitivity and understanding for the mentally and physically challenged and for those who, like our parents, committed themselves to caring for others who were touched by a malady that could easily have been ours.

I was seven years old when Marshall was born. A year or two later when the diagnosis was made, I bought a popular book written by Dale Evans and gave it to our parents. It was called *Angel Unaware*. The title was taken from a verse in the New Testament which says, "Do not neglect to show hospitality to strangers, for thereby some have entertained angels unawares." (Hebrews 13:2) Evans' book was about the Down syndrome child she had with her husband, Roy Rogers.

Roy and Dale named their daughter Robin Elizabeth and their commitment to her (she died at the age of 2) strongly influenced our parents' decision to take care of Marshall, rather than institutionalize him. While it was sometimes difficult for them and later after their death, for me, we never regretted that decision because of the joy Marshall brought to our lives.

In an age when we discard the inconvenient and unwanted in order to pursue pleasure and a life free of burdens, this may seem strange to some. I recall a line from the long-running Broadway musical, *The Fantasticks*: "Deep in December, it's nice to remember, without a hurt the heart is hollow."

Marshall Thomas' "hurts" filled a number of hollow hearts.

At the end of the Christmas classic *It's a Wonderful Life*, George Bailey reads an inscription in a book given to him by Clarence, his guardian angel: "Remember, no man is a failure who has friends."

No life is a failure when it causes so many to care for others. At that my brother succeeded magnificently.

Rachel Maddow and my lesson in civility

By Cal Thomas
February 15, 2012
Tribune Media Services

When one writes about moral convictions, it's probably a good idea to consistently live up to them. That way people can still disagree with your convictions, but they have a difficult time accusing you of hypocrisy.

Last week at the Conservative Political Action Conference (CPAC) in Washington, I failed to live up to one of my highest principles. Here's the background. The story about the Obama administration's attempt to force Catholic and other faith-based institutions to offer employees free contraception in their health care coverage was still fresh. I was asked to be on a panel before what looked like a crowd of about 1,000 conservatives, hungry for "red meat."

A clip was played from Rachel Maddow's MSNBC program. It featured her commenting on the subject. I stupidly said before thinking, "I think she's the best argument in favor of her parents using contraception." I then added, "and all the rest of the crowd at MSNBC, too, for that matter."

It didn't matter that far worse things have been said in print and on TV about me. I am not supposed to behave like that. I co-wrote a book with my liberal Democratic friend, Bob Beckel, called *Common Ground: How to Stop the Partisan War That is Destroying America*. We also write a column together for USA Today. One of the principles in which I believe is not to engage in name-calling; which, to my shame, I did.

The next morning I felt bad about it, so I called Ms. Maddow to apologize. It wasn't one of those meaningless "if I've offended anyone..." apologies; it was heartfelt. I had embarrassed myself and was a bad example to those who read my column and expect better from me.

Maddow could not have been more gracious. She immediately accepted my apology. On her show she said publicly, "I completely believe his apology. I completely accept his apology." To be forgiven by one you have wronged is a blessing, it's even cleansing.

Politics has always been a contact sport. Thomas Jefferson and John Adams went at each other like the worst of enemies, using some of the most outrageous and slanderous language. I don't have bona fides equal to their founding of America, so there is nothing of similar magnitude on which I can fall back.

Maddow also accepted my invitation to lunch and we will soon meet in New York. I am looking forward to it. Since the incident, which, of course, garnered a mini-tornado of media and blogosphere coverage, I have watched a couple of her shows. Without engaging in any qualifiers, she is a strong and competent advocate for her position. Why do so many of us only watch programs that reinforce what we already believe? Where is the growth in that? Whatever else she may or may not be, she is my fellow American.

I have many liberal friends acquired over the years. They are impossible to avoid in the media, but I don't wish to avoid them. They became my friends because I stopped seeing them as labels and began seeing them as persons with innate worth. That is what I failed to do in my first response to Rachel Maddow. One might expect a pro-lifer like me to support the birth of fellow human beings and not suggest they should never have been born.

I expect to like Rachel Maddow because my instinct is to separate the value of a person from his or her political position. For some strange reason (demon possession, perhaps) I failed to do that at CPAC.

So, apology delivered and accepted and lunch will soon be served. I'm trying to decide whose career might be hurt more should someone take a picture of us enjoying a meal and —it is to be hoped, at least by me—each other.

"Who so neglects learning in his youth, loses the past and is dead for the future."
-Euripedes (485-406 B.C.)

LYNNE VARNER

Education, Conversation and Opinions

Lynne Varner of *The Seattle Times* sums up her mission as an op-ed columnist: "My responsibility as a journalist is shining light into dark corners and being the eyes and ears in a community." She notes the difference between an op-ed and metro columnist. "Op-ed is commentary forcibly argued and well-written on any topic. It's another form of commentary similar to a metro column or arts review, but I believe the op-ed strives for a policy-focused broader worldview.

"Part of my task on the opinion page is to take what is happening in Seattle and show how it compares to the rest of the world. I strive to show how our struggles and achievements are universal. This is one of the things that separates us from metro columnists."

For example, the *Seattle Times'* political bloggers and metro columnists wrote extensively about a Washington state ballot initiative regarding charter schools. However, Varner viewed her op-ed column on the same subject as serving a different purpose.

"It is my role to argue the policy imperative, the need to add charters to the potpourri of education reforms changing the landscape of public education. My role is not to delve into the weeds and argue about a single school or school district. When I wrote about charter schools, I shaped my arguments around the national research and what would be best for the one million school kids in Washington State, where a public education system struggles to serve everyone."

Her attraction to having a public platform began in college when

Varner heard a guest speaker, Cathy Hughes, founder of Radio One (a company of 53 broadcast stations) speak of her motivation to become rich and powerful enough to affect change. Later, Varner worked as a reporter for *United Press International*, and, subsequently *The Washington Post.*

She relocated to work at *The Seattle Times* as a reporter and eventually added op-ed columnist to her duties. "I knew that I wanted to go to the opinion side eventually. It's not about being wealthy—no one gets rich in journalism—but having a forum. I've covered politics, local, state and county government, the cops' beat, and so I knew I could bring a well-rounded background to opinion writing."

Her column appears every other Friday in *The Seattle Times*, but she writes daily for the opinion page's blog, *Ed Cetera.* She also serves on her newspaper's editorial board and submits four to five times a week unsigned editorials that represent the views of the newspaper. Varner received a Pulitzer nomination in 2006 for a series of columns about the U.S. Supreme Court's review of Seattle's use of racial preferences in public education.

From her early career days as a journalist, a passion for education grew. "I write about everything, but I am most interested in education. I've managed to broaden the intersection of poverty, race, gender and criminal justice because it all comes out of education; what we are doing or not doing. Even if I were to cover the environmental beat, I would bring it back to the classroom."

Her op-ed column is a personal portrait. "I can't shy away from who I am and how that informs my thinking. I'm an African American woman who grew up on the East Coast. I don't have a small town sensibility, and I have a particular interest in children of color. Having written about education and poverty, I know up close about having a choice, and the impact the right to choose can have. Let's talk about this.

"I grew up without a father, so I'm interested in the struggles of single-parent households and in the difference having two parents can make in a child's life. I'm interested in charter schools because they are structured in a way that forces parents and students to care about education. For one, you have to apply for admission, and as a parent you have to actually take an interest in your children's education. Many charters require parents to volunteer or commit in some other way.

"Charter schools, why do I care so much about this issue? It is a key part of the public education system and I know that education is key to critical things in life, a good job, a home, a stable family and income. As a country, we have invested in social programs and efforts to help people in terms of housing, health and employment—all kinds of help for people who face disadvantages. But there has not been a purposeful, all-out push on education. It's about education, not another social program.

"I'm a Democrat, and I think government plays a role in ensuring equality, but I think the equality comes from kids walking in and saying, 'Hire me because I'm good.' 'It's about keeping them engaged in school and making them believe there is another way out. Gathering knowledge will immunize you against the forces that can land you in prison.

"Like it or not, our society is built on racial dynamics. I'm in journalism so that I can apply those dynamics to reality, not to the stereotypes. I bring a different voice and a unique perspective."

Varner sees her column as a catalyst for conversation and, as such, feels her signature writing style is conversational, and feels the "I have spoken" approach by other writers is off-putting. An authoritarian tone is not what Varner uses in her personal life, so it is not a natural fit in her professional life either.

"I want people to think I sat down in a booth with them, picked up my glass of wine, and said, 'I want to tell you what's on my mind. I have an opinion, but I'm willing to listen.' People might tell me, 'You didn't think of this or that aspect in your column,' and I'd say,

'You're right. I didn't. That's for you to bring up because this is a two-way conversation.'"

What are ways to break into this field for freelance columnists if they didn't start, as she did, with a reporting background?

"Papers are attracted to people who come with their own audiences; they already have people who are interested in what they think.

"Every media outlet is looking to grow its audience. You have to be a really sharp, astute thinker with a built-in audience. We're so hungry to capture new markets and hold on to old ones, and we are looking for people to help us. It's about branding. Outlets are always looking for new brands because that new brand will bring in a new audience.

"The challenge is budget. Papers are not doing a lot of hiring, but even in the midst of layoffs on the editorial page, we are expanding in key areas. We want to find people who can shore us up, particularly with online and multimedia platforms like video and visual work. We want to do more of that and we want to do it better. We need people who know their way around short films and video, people who are good at building online audiences through Twitter, Facebook, or their own blogs. If they're getting advertising for it, then they've reached that magic number of readers that makes them attractive to us."

Lynne Varner's Writing Process, Insights and Advice

Know your power and really care about an issue. "That's the first thing. I have to hear or read about something and have it stick with me. I walk around and I'm still angry, or sad, or concerned about it. Also, I know that I have something to say and I'm the best person to say it. I can get lawmakers to listen or to call out to the community in a way no one else can."

Use examples that help readers visualize your point. "The most important thing is to illustrate exactly what you are talking about. I like to use examples that will make people say, 'I get that. I see it now.' I address issues head on. My first graph lays out my opinion, and then my column goes into backing it up. I don't want readers to say, 'What the heck is she talking about?'"

Be firm in your position. Op-ed columnists do not have to present both sides. Take a clear stand. "You are not allowed to have two hands as a columnist. You can't write, 'on one hand, but on the other hand…' This is muddled writing. Be forceful. I pop out and say this is what I believe."

Be tenacious. "You can't do 'one-off's' all the time. To be a good opinion writer, you have to write a body of work on an issue. What you are saying is 'these are my principles' and you return to them again and again. I'm going to find one hundred different ways to say what I believe."

One column cannot cover it all. On an issue Varner presents her information and is comfortable knowing that more is likely to emerge. "I have not read everything on a topic, and knowing other people will raise more research is fine with me. Creating public discussion is the point. Here's what I think, what do you think?"

A minor happening can be part of a big-picture issue. "I wrote about Ivan, a gorilla who died in captivity, because I've long been interested in the debate about whether we should keep animals locked up in zoos. I'm sad for Ivan, but I grabbed onto him because I wanted to revisit the ethical dilemmas faced by zoos."

<u>Push past the fear</u>. It's what a writer must do regularly to make a difference as an op-ed columnist. Battling opponents is only part of it. Often it is more difficult to push past the inner voices that natter, "You can't do this," or "C'mon! You're not that good and you never will be." Varner said, "It takes an undue amount of courage."

<u>Do the Columbo thing</u>. Getting sources to talk or digging up information can be difficult for any journalist, the Freedom of Information Act notwithstanding. Varner said, "I have perseverance, I have empathy in situations that call for it, and I do a little Colombo thing, where I say, 'I'm pretty sure what I'm asking for is public information by law, isn't it?'"

Actor Peter Falk played a rumpled homicide detective in the TV series, *Colombo*. He solved murders mainly by disarming witnesses by being bumbling and awkward. Suspects underestimated him because he appeared unassuming, friendly and a bit absent-minded. It was a classic case of being dumb like a fox.

Varner is neither awkward nor absentminded, but like Colombo, she is down-to-earth and approachable when talking to sources. "I'm looking for information in their heads. I'm honest with people and tell them exactly why I'm interested in this information. I want to know both sides, and I don't mind showing them my hand, as in, this is what I'm thinking about this issue. What are you thinking?"

In her columns, it is important to Varner that readers know exactly where she stands on an issue.

"I do the reporting and present my argument in a way that makes readers take away the most salient point of what I'm writing. I'm always thinking about that nut graph in my head; what I want them to be talking about with their friends, when someone asks, 'Did you read Varner's column today?'"

Trayvon Martin: moving beyond one teen's death

By Lynne Varner
Tuesday, April 3, 2012
Seattle Times

I've run out of patience with armchair jurists looking to justify the killing of Florida teen Trayvon Martin.

They must stop trying to find a justification where none exists. Geraldo Rivera has apologized for asserting that Martin wearing his sweatshirt with the hood up was as much to blame for his death as the shooter, George Zimmerman.

For anyone else who subscribes to the hoodie defense theory, the 17-year-old was walking down the street with his hood up because it was *raining*. It was a hood, not a target.

Martin's teenage behavioral lapses, including suspension from school for having a bag containing marijuana residue, are trotted out in a further effort to place some of the blame on his own dead shoulders. But the facts get in the way of that live-by-the sword-die by-it explanation: Martin was walking down the street, chatting on a cell phone with his girl, armed only with a can of iced tea and a bag of Skittles—all legal under our Constitution—when he fell under the suspicion of a self-appointed neighborhood watch captain.

Isn't it curious that a country so progressive it elected a black president can so easily regress back to tired stereotypes about young black men and clothing choices?

A kid was shot to death because he *looked* dangerous and we almost didn't give a damn. The public almost bought without question the self-defense claim by Zimmerman, a guy with a history of aggressive behavior whose most common photograph is a mug shot taken when he was arrested in 2005 for assaulting a police officer.

We almost let a shoddy investigation stand as fact and Trayvon Martin's death filed under "tragic but understandable."

Thankfully, Tracy Martin and Sybrina Fulton refused to let their son go out like that. Since the February shooting, they've waged a battle joined by many around the world to raise questions authorities should have been asking.

Here's one: why was the dead kid tested for drugs and alcohol but the living man who shot him not tested? Here's another: why did Martin's body lay unidentified in a morgue for two days when anyone could've picked up his cell phone—the one he was talking on before he died—and trace his identity.

Martin's parents are not demanding an eye for an eye, they're asking for a full investigation, a basic principle of our justice system.

It's tempting to blame Florida's Stand Your Ground law and the broad leeway it offers to self-defense claims. And don't get me started on the proliferation of weapons that has practically everyone and their Pug packing heat. The shooting deaths of Korean-American college students in California this week is a tragic example of how easy it remains to get a gun.

But Martin's death is a powerful reminder of how vulnerable we all are. Who knows how we, or our children, fit into some idiot's stereotype? A change of demographics and he could be any of our sons.

And the racial dynamics of America show that more often than not, he will be African American.

FBI statistics show blacks are the victims of hate crimes at much higher rates than any other ethnic group in the United States. African Americans are 12.6 percent of the U.S. population, but they made up 70 percent of the victims of racial hate crimes in 2010.

A Harvard University-sponsored website, Project Implicit, offers clues about what's going on. One can go to implicit.harvard.edu/implicit/demo/featuredtask.html and take a test that measures racial biases. The results are unsurprising.

Negative views of blacks stand out, even among some black test takers.

I'm confident justice is coming in the Martin case. But the movement his death has launched must continue beyond this one death to a wholesale look at how America views the murders of black men. We don't take them or their pain seriously. And we absolutely should.

Why it's a good idea for Seattle's students to talk about racial preferences

By Lynne K. Varner
March 7, 2013
Seattle Times

A Seattle Public Schools class explores sexism and white privilege. The latter topic is so politically loaded district officials recently convened a committee to examine the course content.

The district's action puzzles me. America was built on a system of racial exclusions thriving well into the 20th century. Facts are facts. Surely we can all talk about that.

Yes, the term "white privilege" is a provocative description of the "Citizenship and Social Justice" class at the Center School. But the shorthand rings true.

How it is discussed is critical. No need to make people who came of age long after segregation feel guilty about the second-class citizenship once conferred upon African Americans.

Guilt is pointless. Understanding the ways history continues to cast a long shadow on today is the better goal.

A contemporary example is in the Seattle Public Schools, where African-American students are suspended and expelled at three to four times the rate of nonblack students. A federal investigation is under way.

Disparities in the district's disciplinary rates are neither surprising nor new. A Times story written in 2001 started out this way:

"Acknowledging that students of different races sometimes are disciplined differently for the same offenses, Seattle public-school officials are calling for sharper definitions of 'disobedience,' 'disruptive conduct' and 'rule-breaking.'"

Some things don't change. Nor is it only Seattle struggling with uneven treatment and opportunities for kids of color. The feds are simply looking our way.

Around a year ago this time, I wrote about the shooting death of Florida teen Trayvon Martin and how it fueled talks with my son about racial biases. The U.S. Department of Education's statistics showing that black students nationwide are disciplined at higher rates and with harsher penalties has spurred another conversation with my child about the need to be beyond reproach at school.

My son is both his own person and a member of an ethnic group that is often judged by its pathologies rather than by the traits of its individuals.

When comedian Bill Cosby advises African Americans to work hard, build stable families and strive for success, he's reinforcing work in progress. But the public perception is that Cosby's remarks are a futile attempt to keep a race of 30 million people from self-destructing.

And so my husband and I give our son a talk that is a blend of Cosby and the Seattle white-privilege course.

We tell him that the art of school discipline is subjective.

Discrimination has been outlawed, but old biases may remain. Some people will judge him based on skin color, his manner of dress or the timbre and emotion in his voice.

We tell our son not only does he not want to make trouble, he doesn't want to be *near* it lest he get mistaken for the instigator.

We tell him that respect is in the eye of the beholder. He may think he's being respectful by avoiding looking teachers directly in the eye or speaking frankly of classroom dilemmas, but a teacher may see and hear insolence.

As my son grows taller and more masculine, I'm reminded of how teaching remains an overwhelmingly white, female profession. And so we tell him never, ever, ever do anything that could appear remotely threatening.

Sure, some adults need to question their perceptions. But it won't happen in time to save him from detention or suspension.

Yes, it is a social tightrope that he must walk, one many adults have trouble navigating.

But we tell our son we believe in his ability to do it successfully.

And those statistics showing the high rate of black students getting kicked out of school?

Our efforts are to ensure he doesn't become another statistic.

"Television is an invention that permits you to be entertained in your living room by people you wouldn't have in your home."
-David Frost

JOANNA WEISS

When Pop Culture Meets Politics

Joanna Weiss of *The Boston Globe* sums up her career: "Opinion journalist, TV and radio commentator, public speaker, social media maven, pop culture guru, political junkie. Always looking for stories to tell." Pop culture as mirrored in politics is her unique viewpoint.

"At least half of my columns are about pop culture, and I like to write about what in our society is reflected in political culture. Putting together these two things may seem separate, but in my mind, they are very connected. You can't have one without the other, and how that plays out and is reflected in political culture is my particular niche," said Weiss whose 700-word column runs twice weekly.

She defines pop culture broadly. "It's what's on TV, in the movies, in the media. It's also about social media, how people are using Facebook, Twitter, and technology. I would define it as entertainment writ large that we consume and that we produce.

"There was a time when people thought op-ed should be serious and policy oriented, but I think it's about offering opinions about things that matter. I would define it as broadly as that. Who is to tell me what doesn't matter?"

She is her audience. "I write mostly for myself, to answer questions that I have when I read the news or look at the world."

Unlike many national news organizations *The Boston Globe* staff has parity between male and female columnists, although the topics of

Weiss' column fall along the expected lines of gender and social issues. She believes the goal of an op-ed columnist is, fundamentally, to offer an informed view of current events. Equally important is her conviction to put pressure on those with authority and the government.

"We have an editorial board of people who write opinions and columns. We meet four days a week and discuss issues of the day. We come up with an interesting mix."

Weiss began her career in 1994 as a local government reporter for *The Times Picayune* in New Orleans, her first job out of college. In 1999, she relocated to be a metro reporter at *The Boston Globe*. Since she enjoyed pop culture so much, Weiss added entertainment critic to her list of writing duties but she never intended to become an op-ed columnist. The suggestion came from Peter S. Cannellos, one of her first editors at *The Globe* who later became chief of the paper's Washington Bureau. Eventually, she brought together her passions for entertainment and politics in her op-ed column.

"When you are a critic it is a form of opinion writing. I found I wanted to tie what I was watching on TV to what was going on in society and politics. What I wrote for the entertainment section started to blur the lines with news because I had a foot in both worlds. It's unusual in newspapers. Typically, you take one track or the other, but I did both."

For example, one of her columns starts with actress Angelina Jolie famously flashing her leg at the Oscars and then delves into the politics of abortion. "It [leg flashing at the Oscars] happened at the time the state legislature in Virginia would consider a bill that would require women to have an ultrasound before getting an abortion. The bill couldn't move forward because legislators didn't want to say the word 'vagina.'

"I wrote a column about how much we talk about sex, but when it comes to legislating things that will involve our lives, we can't even say the word. How can we create policy when we can't even talk about it?"

Her goal is to expand a reader's thinking as well as public discourse.

"I would like people to make connections that they would not have otherwise made. That is something I can contribute to a public policy debate. I'm not an economics expert, or a scientist, or have a technical expertise in certain fields, but a journalist's job is to piece things together. A columnist should be able to pull together things from different parts of the world and put them together to help people see things a little differently."

Joanna Weiss's Writing Process, Insights, and Advice

Curiosity should be a columnist's number one trait.

Be conversational, not preachy or strident.

Pare the writing down and strive for clarity.

Humor, if appropriate, and self-deprecation are reminders of our humanity.

Develop a recognizable "voice," which is your personality and writing style.

Use statistics sparingly. Use one killer stat that makes the reader gasp.

Writer's block is a sign that more reporting/research needs to be done.

Evoke emotion, but tread lightly. Avoid being maudlin or manipulative. Weiss recalled writing about a Palestinian boy living in Israel who was gravely ill with a kidney malfunction. Surgery at Boston's Children's Hospital was his only hope, but his family had no money. Jewish philanthropists came to his rescue and paid for his care.

"Lay it out and just tell the story. The emotion comes with it. Don't milk it. The facts spoke for themselves and I didn't have to do more than that," Weiss said.

Accept that a 700-word column cannot say it all. Therefore, keep it simple. The goal is to change the public conversation, not to win everyone over to your side. There will always be aspects to a topic that cannot be covered within a limited space.

Readers often chastise Weiss for not addressing this or that on any given subject. She advised, "You don't have to make a legal, airtight case. You just have to make a good argument. Take a debate and inject a few ideas and connections that people haven't thought about before. Send everyone off on an interesting tangent."

Crafting opinion columns that ring with intelligence and offer a fresh perspective is hard work. Every writer undergoes an emotional process toward fully owning his or her public declarations, and Weiss noted, "In the end, it's my column, which makes it both terrifying and liberating."

The Help: America Pats Itself on the Back

By Joanna Weiss
August 16, 2011
Globe Newspaper Company

It's hardly surprising that *The Help* did wonders at the box office last weekend. The movie about beleaguered maids and Southern belles in Jackson, Mississippi, is funny and moving, with some beautiful performances. And it's the definition of a crowd-pleaser: A film that lets us pat ourselves on the back over how far we've come.

Yes, America, we can all look back on Mississippi, circa 1963, and agree on these bold principles: Racism is bad! Racists are bad! Separate outdoor bathrooms for black maids are bad! Now, let's head on home!

Based on the bestselling novel by Kathryn Stockett, *The Help* is the story of Skeeter, a young white debutante who, like her friends, was raised by a kindly black maid while her mother was busy with the Junior League. When Skeeter returns home from college, it occurs to her that these maids have, in fact, lived difficult lives. Also, she wants a job with a New York publisher who happens to be keen on the maids' stories. So Skeeter interviews the maids, then puts their anonymous tales into a best-selling book that brings enlightenment to several other white people.

The story has an element of truth to it; Stockett grew up in Jackson in the 70s and 80s, and was raised by a loving black maid who wore a uniform and used an outdoor toilet in the blistering heat.

But in the book and the movie, the action takes place in 1963, in the heart of the civil rights era. The maids' travails—painful, Jim Crow-era hardship and humiliation—are juxtaposed with the Medgar Evers slaying. John F. Kennedy dies. Bob Dylan plays in the background. It's two-and-a-half hours of wallowing in battles that have already been fought and won: an all-American cop-out.

This isn't a call for self-flagellation; we should feel proud of the progress our nation has made in a short period of time. A movie whose villains are pretty young racists would have been much less of a gimme 50 years ago. But if we've lost most of our tolerance for stark discrimination, we've moved onto different battles, over subtler ills: embedded prejudices, achievement gaps, structural inequalities. The modern dynamics of race and class are more nuanced, more challenging, less guaranteed to yield box office gold.

The Help flirts with some of those deeper ideas, such as the social dynamic when poor women raise rich children as their own, then become their employees. But the movie doesn't delve very far. With a couple of exceptions, the white women here don't seem conflicted so much as oblivious, cartoonishly callous, and mean. And boy, do they get their comeuppance: Hilly, the meanest and most racist of the debs, winds up with a stern talking-to and a really ugly cold sore on her lip—plus the bloodthirsty hoots of the movie theater crowds.

It's no wonder that they cheer. Americans are always looking for quick fixes and reasons to hang the "Mission Accomplished" banner. And it's easy to judge the present against the past: *Mad Men* started off with a similar trick, letting us sneer at the sexist 60s through the lens of women's lib.

We also yearn for validation, some proof that good intentions make a difference. Barack Obama won the presidency for many reasons, but one of them was symbolism: People felt good about the idea that a black man could win. During the 2008 primaries, my brother told me he was voting for Obama because Hillary Clinton would draw the same old partisan rancor. Obama would surely herald an era of calm and mature debate. The following year, I asked my brother how that was working out.

On the other hand, with the exception of some particularly race-related sideshows—the birther absurdity springs to mind—Obama's current political predicament is actually a sign of how far we've come—not just since 1963, but since 2008. He's not only the first black president now; he's also just the president, capable of plenty of misjudgments and mistakes. If he wins or loses in 2012, it will be largely on his merits, his actions, his ability to translate ideas into a campaign. That's not Hollywood-caliber drama, but it's progress.

After Steubenville, a short and sweet response

By Joanna Weiss
March 27, 2013
Globe Newspaper Company

Sometimes the best ideas stem from procrastination. While studying for finals at the University of Oregon last week, Samantha Stendal, a 19-year-old sophomore, was following news coverage of the Steubenville, Ohio, rape trial, in which two high school football players were convicted of assaulting a drunken 16-year-old girl.

Stendal grew frustrated at the talk about alcohol, the suggestion that assault is a sad-but-inevitable byproduct of partying, the regrets over promising lives cut short by unfortunate "mistakes."

"I was reading so much on the victim-blaming and 'rape culture,'" Stendler, a film major, told me by phone this week. "I needed to see something positive on the Internet...And I knew that I could make something."

So in between tests, she scribbled out a rough storyboard. The day after finals, she gathered some friends to shoot a 25 second, which she posted to YouTube a few days later under the title "A Needed Response."

It's a shot of a guy in a T-shirt, standing in front of a couch on which a woman is apparently asleep. "Hey, bros," he says to the camera. "Check who passed out on the couch. Guess what I'm going to do to her."

He proceeds to put a pillow under her head, a blanket over her body, a cup of tea on a table beside her. Then he turns to the camera again and says, "Real men treat women with respect."

Over and out and there you have it: The most concise, useful addition I've seen in awhile to this old, sad conversation about alcohol, sex, and safety. It's unsurprising that the video quickly went viral—or that, on its YouTube page and beyond, another long and vicious conversation has unspooled about sluts and feminists, blame and responsibility, the fact that sometimes men get attacked, and sometimes women aren't nice.

I know, I know; Internet commenters, in all of their anonymous glory, are not a useful barometer for humanity. Still, it goes to show how hard it is, on the ever-fraught subject of sex and consent, to get rid of this arms race of blame—this notion that, in order to call someone's behavior unacceptable, you are somehow obligated to point out problematic behavior from the other side.

There have been, in recent years, a lot of clever responses to that line of thinking. A series of "Slut Walk" rallies have countered police suggestions that women should watch what they wear, to somehow stave off assault. This week, people are having fun with the Twitter hashtag #safetytipsforladies—apparently launched by a woman in Australia who was incensed by a newspaper commentary over the difference between "victim-blaming" or "risk management."

(Among the most retweeted quips: "If you hide your forearms in your sleeves, the rapist will mistake you for a T-Rex and carry on his way." Also: "Don't be attacked by guys with a promising future. That is the absolute WORST decision you can make.")

But there's something equally refreshing about the earnestness of Stendal's video, which removes the charged language and the justifiable anger, and introduces the kind of blissfully simple idea that high school and college students should be able to understand. If kids were truly trained to respect each other's boundaries—to treat other people with basic human decency—maybe we wouldn't be having these conversations quite so often.

It's not that people aren't trying. A few years ago, public health officials in Edmonton, Alberta, pioneered a public service campaign called "Don't Be That Guy": a series of posters, to be hung in restrooms in bars, with such slogans as "Just because she isn't saying no doesn't mean she's saying yes."

And recently, someone launched a petition, on the White House webpage, to make the definition of "consent" a mandatory part of sex education in public schools.

That's a lovely idea, but also sad: that we should need some kind of government mandate to teach kids the difference between "yes" and the absence of "yes," the difference between hurting someone and helping her.

These aren't difficult concepts, after all. A 25-second video takes care of things quite nicely.

"For courage mounteth with occasion."
-William Shakespeare (*King John*)

THE OCCASIONAL OP-ED CONTRIBUTOR

Excellent writing can make a difference, whether an opinion column is published once, or it appears four times a week all year round. It's the alchemy of personality, background, experiences, and gifted expression.

For those who aspire to a regular byline, perseverance is a practice. Stay the course. Regroup and attack from another angle. Endure. Keep at it day after day.

But then, there is the occasional contributor, one who is compelled to write by sudden circumstance or experience. Such writers might be one-hit wonders, but boy! They knock it right out of the park. Angelina Jolie is an actress and director, and writing op-ed is not a primary aspect of her career. Yet her editorial about her medical decision to get a preventative double mastectomy was powerful both in its vulnerability and education. If she never wrote another column, this one surely will endure.

When most meaningful, opinion writing is about sparking public discussion and letting others know they are not alone.

My Medical Choice

By Angelina Jolie
May 14, 2013
The New York Times

My mother fought cancer for almost a decade and died at 56. She
held out long enough to meet the first of her grandchildren and to
hold them in her arms. But my other children will never have the
chance to know her and experience how loving and gracious she
was.

We often speak of "Mommy's mommy," and I find myself trying to
explain the illness that took her away from us. They have asked if
the same could happen to me. I have always told them not to worry,
but the truth is I carry a "faulty" gene, BRCA1, which sharply
increases my risk of developing breast cancer and ovarian cancer.
My doctors estimated that I had an 87 percent risk of breast cancer
and a 50 percent risk of ovarian cancer, although the risk is different
in the case of each woman.

Only a fraction of breast cancers result from an inherited gene
mutation. Those with a defect in BRCA1 have a 65 percent risk of
getting it, on average.

Once I knew that this was my reality, I decided to be proactive and
to minimize the risk as much I could. I made a decision to have a
preventive double mastectomy. I started with the breasts, as my risk
of breast cancer is higher than my risk of ovarian cancer, and the
surgery is more complex.

On April 27, I finished the three months of medical procedures that
the mastectomies involved. During that time I have been able to keep
this private and to carry on with my work.

But I am writing about it now because I hope that other women can
benefit from my experience. Cancer is still a word that strikes fear
into people's hearts, producing a deep sense of powerlessness. But

today it is possible to find out through a blood test whether you are highly susceptible to breast and ovarian cancer, and then take action.

My own process began on Feb. 2 with a procedure known as a "nipple delay," which rules out disease in the breast ducts behind the nipple and draws extra blood flow to the area. This causes some pain and a lot of bruising, but it increases the chance of saving the nipple.

Two weeks later I had the major surgery, where the breast tissue is removed and temporary fillers are put in place. The operation can take eight hours. You wake up with drain tubes and expanders in your breasts. It does feel like a scene out of a science-fiction film. But days after surgery you can be back to a normal life.

Nine weeks later, the final surgery is completed with the reconstruction of the breasts with an implant. There have been many advances in this procedure in the last few years, and the results can be beautiful.

I wanted to write this to tell other women that the decision to have a mastectomy was not easy. But it is one I am very happy that I made. My chances of developing breast cancer have dropped from 87 percent to under 5 percent. I can tell my children that they don't need to fear they will lose me to breast cancer.

It is reassuring that they see nothing that makes them uncomfortable. They can see my small scars and that's it. Everything else is just Mommy, the same as she always was. And they know that I love them and will do anything to be with them as long as I can. On a personal note, I do not feel any less of a woman. I feel empowered that I made a strong choice that in no way diminishes my femininity.

I am fortunate to have a partner, Brad Pitt, who is so loving and supportive. So to anyone who has a wife or girlfriend going through this, know that you are a very important part of the transition. Brad was at the Pink Lotus Breast Center, where I was treated, for every minute of the surgeries. We managed to find moments to laugh together. We knew this was the right thing to do for our family and that it would bring us closer. And it has.

For any woman reading this, I hope it helps you to know you have options. I want to encourage every woman, especially if you have a family history of breast or ovarian cancer, to seek out the information and medical experts who can help you through this aspect of your life, and to make your own informed choices.

I acknowledge that there are many wonderful holistic doctors working on alternatives to surgery. My own regimen will be posted in due course on the Web site of the Pink Lotus Breast Center. I hope that this will be helpful to other women.

Breast cancer alone kills some 458,000 people each year, according to the World Health Organization, mainly in low- and middle-income countries. It has got to be a priority to ensure that more women can access gene testing and lifesaving preventive treatment, whatever their means and background, wherever they live. The cost of testing for BRCA1 and BRCA2, at more than $3,000 in the United States, remains an obstacle for many women.

I choose not to keep my story private because there are many women who do not know that they might be living under the shadow of cancer. It is my hope that they, too, will be able to get gene tested, and that if they have a high risk they, too, will know that they have strong options.

Life comes with many challenges. The ones that should not scare us are the ones we can take on and take control of.

"It is inexcusable for scientists to torture animals; let them make their experiments on journalists and politicians."
-Henrik Ibsen (1828-1906)

HATE MAIL

Hate mail is hurled at opinion writers. Angry emails (often sent from those who cannot spell) condemn the columnist's intelligence, background, and sanity. At times the missives can be hilarious, but often they are just cruel and mean spirited. Even worse are the stalkers and death threats, frightening and real.

Professional columnists respect constructive dialogue, and even aggressive critics will make fair points. Such responses are very different from the haters who seek only to attack and insult.

The op-ed columnist is targeted in the public's crosshairs every week. Accepting that slings and arrows of criticism shower the territory does not grant emotional immunity. Stress and fear can be debilitating. Not surprisingly, many writers said, "That's why God created the delete button."

Yet dealing with relentless negativity on a daily basis can be an art. Long time columnists each have a personal approach to managing the poison.

Kathleen Parker

"As a columnist you are exposing the limits of your own intellect. You're sticking your head above the fray when you do that, and people try to knock it off.

"You can't believe the things people write to me. I delete it pretty quickly because it's bad for my psyche. I'm not going to expose myself to vileness on purpose.

"When I first started, I used to collect them. It was back when people communicated by handwritten letters, snail mail. There was no email. We'd sit around at my house and I'd read them aloud to my husband and sons, and they'd get a big laugh. My husband especially loved it when they'd question his manhood because clearly, it was evidence that I was not getting what I needed from a man!

"My son said, 'Mom, why do you care what people think?' and I thought, 'Oh, you're right!'

"My cure for hate mail now is just to go to a mall. I walk around and think, 'Whose opinion in this crowd do I value?' and that makes me feel better right away."

Michael R. Masterson

"Hate mail is part of the game. There's no way to become a columnist that has credibility without hate mail. You're going to step on toes. I've had more than hate mail. The windows of my car and my house were shot out.

"[A different episode] When I was leaving Arkansas with my family to work at *The Los Angeles Times*, I heard that the sheriff and his deputies were waiting to set me up. They were going to search the car, drop a bag and get the last laugh on possession charges. I told a good friend of mine with the State Police what I'd heard, and he came and escorted us over the county line. Sure enough, there were four sheriff's deputies in cars waiting out there.

"I've had hate mail from the beginning. After 42 years, I've been called every name you can think of. When you report what you believe to be the truth, the truth steps on toes. When prominent people are crossed, you can expect to get some pushback.

"When someone starts screaming at you in writing, they are not trying to deal rationally or reasonably, and I just put it in the trash. If they sound dangerous, then I make a call to some authority and let them have it for their files.

"Hate mail is a distasteful part of the business. It all boils down to expectations. I expect it, so it doesn't slow me down or stop me from writing. I've gotten hateful letters and phone calls. 'You better watch your back, or 'you're in trouble,' or "you don't know what you're taking on.' I just say, 'Thanks for calling,' hang up and go on. You have to be able to put that stuff in its own little space in your mind and heart and realize that it's part of the game.

"If you want to write an opinion, then you better have an opinion, and it better be credible, and if it's credible you're going to irritate a certain number of people."

Joel Brinkley

"Like every columnist—every journalist for that matter—I get a lot of hate mail. *The New York Times* based me in Israel for four years, and I learned that when you write about Israel and the Palestinians you always get harsh criticism from one side or the other—or both. More than from anyplace else, it seemed.

"I still write frequent columns about the Middle East and get a dozen or more angry emails each time. I've learned to let it roll off my back. It doesn't bother me. Sometimes though, when I get a hate-filled note, I am moved to write back, saying: "Well, aren't you a tendentious fellow?" That usually ends it.

"But then in early 2013, I was in Vietnam and wrote about the nation's dietary habits—their propensity to eat nearly all of their wildlife. I and the people traveling with me noted there were few birds or other animals anywhere to be seen. I did some research and found that the World Wildlife Fund describes the state as the world's greatest wildlife malefactor. And I saw that, a few months earlier, Conservation International had reported that several varieties of the Vietnamese gibbon, part of the ape family, 'are perilously close to extinction'—all but a few of them already eaten. That struck me as a pretty good column.

"Little did I know, the Vietnamese, not the Israelis, appear to be the most sensitive people on earth. They hated the column, even though it was perfectly accurate. I got volumes of hate mail unlike anything I had ever experienced in my life—even when reporting abroad as a newspaper foreign correspondent. They called me ignorant and a racist.

"One blogger wrote: "Joel Brinkley finds out that, these days, the truth itself is racist."

"A fellow who described himself as 'a former Fullbrighter in Vietnam' sent me a note so filled with vile insults and invective that I couldn't help myself. I wrote back to him and asked why he thought being a 'former Fullbrighter' gave him the right to send me an email filled with insults and profanity?

"Little did I know that right away he would start a petition on Change.org to have me fired from my job. Over a month it got more than 5,000 signatures, mostly from Vietnamese and Vietnamese-Americans. But, fortunately, I'm still here.

"Looking back on it, I often think I shouldn't be deterred from writing more about Vietnam. I shouldn't let them scare me off.

"Thus far I haven't."

Lynne Varner

"You need to be fearless because hate mail can be debilitating. It can make you do the worst thing: pull your punches. You have to be on guard with that.

"Some people have been emailing me for 10 years. They can be scary, some racist or personal. I block them. There's a guy who's been emailing me for years and wants to prove that he is not being racist when he says that black kids are trouble or that black crime is ruining America.

"Race becomes this abbreviation for what some people want to load it up with, a dangerous situation or whatever. I've been called a 'whiner,' and whiner seems to be attached to those who write about civil rights, or women who write about equality.

"Something solely dropped into the laps of columnists of color, especially black columnists, is that we are playing the race card. It's like they're saying, 'We've elected a black president so you can stop talking about it.' People say, 'So you think you haven't progressed?' Of course we have, but we are not yet there because there is no way you can wave a magic wand and be made whole, and many will stop thinking their ugly thoughts.

"The troll factor has risen tenfold, and it's amazing how bold and vitriolic they can be, hiding behind a computer screen and logging on with a fake name. The online comments, the ones beneath my blog, I don't read them. They make my husband furious, but I don't read them. It can ruin my day, but if it can make me shy away from a topic, then it lets the other side win. I can't do that. It's my responsibility not to shut up and go away."

Ellen Goodman

Despite breaking ground in her field almost four decades ago, Goodman observes parity for female columnists still does not exist and suspects the criticism and hate mail that dog opinion columnists deter many women.

Goodman said, "There are so many angry voices out there and not that many women want to be in the middle of a food fight. One of the things that happen to women when they get into this hardball atmosphere is that you are inevitably attacked.

"After all, you are telling people what you think, and then they tell you what they think about what you think. You definitely have to develop some toughness about criticism. After all, what is criticism?

It's not cancer, it's just criticism.

"I will definitely read people who disagree with me and respond to them very politely, but hate mail? Why would anybody read that?" Negative reader response comes with the territory, and anyone who writes to make a difference accepts that condition and should set personal boundaries. Goodman believes the power to make a columnist feel bad is not an automatic permission that goes with a tagline and an email address. Decide whose opinion you value and disregard the rest.

Robert C. Koehler

"Detractors are part of the fun. It means I've disturbed the universe when someone disagrees, and disagreement is not necessarily hate mail. Respectful letters of disagreement are wonderful things to receive.

"If an email is really mean spirited ('You're an asshole') then I won't respond, but I keep all of my emails.

"For the most part, let it sit. I don't respond right away when I'm emotionally triggered because I almost always regret it. A pissing contest ensues and it's ridiculous. I always thank people for writing and I thank them for reading something they disagree with. It's what free speech is all about, so thank you for that, and then I address the issue.

"I will respond to challenges and disagreements. Sometimes it will totally turn things around, and they will thank me for replying and we will have a respectful dialogue.

"All hate mail has an element of wonder for me. It means they read it in a newspaper! If they read it online, they read it for free and they are probably progressives who would agree with me. But by and large, angry letters mean they saw my column in a newspaper and that means they paid to read it. So I'm already predisposed to be happy about hate mail."

Connie Schultz

"If it's very ugly, I just delete it. You don't have to deal with anonymous vitriol, it's like subjecting yourself to abuse."

What Schultz finds more disturbing than personal attacks is the hate mail leveled at the everyday folks featured in her stories. The widespread unidentified postings as allowed by many newspapers have subjected them to cruel public comments.

For example, Connie wrote about a union man whose long time company relocated and left him jobless. He later committed suicide, and when Schultz's column ran, readers posted hateful comments about the man. His daughter who gave Connie the details about her father's story, called sobbing over the consequences.

Schultz recalled, "Her mother told her, 'Don't bother coming home.' The comments were so awful: 'What kind of Christian would shoot himself in the head?' 'What kind of man wouldn't work at Walmart?'

"I couldn't take down the comments. I had no control over them, and it was going to change how I write columns. After all this time of trying to tell real life stories, in this new world of online vitriol you have to protect them [the subjects of her columns]. It's on a case-by-case basis, but I don't name them as often as I used to. It does hurt the work, but I don't want to subject people to that."

Derrick Z. Jackson

"One of the benefits of digital America is that hate mail no longer comes in the mail. In earlier days, I'd get written hate mail through the slot at my home. There were one or two occasions when my family was threatened.

"If hate mail is ridiculous with racial slurs, I just throw it away. Hate mail by definition is irrational, slur laced ranting, and not worthy of consideration. Now I get screeds from people online, but I can delete them.

"I let it roll it off my shoulders. When I was hired at *The Milwaukee Journal* as a high school reporter, my first story didn't go well and one of the editors told me, 'I don't think you're going to make it.'

"Larry Whiteside took me aside. He was one of the first African-American beat writers covering baseball for a major U.S. newspaper. [In 2008 Whiteside was inducted into the sportswriters' wing of the Baseball Hall of Fame]. He said to me, 'It's going to be OK. Let me show you something.'

"He opened his drawer and it was filled with hate mail from people who couldn't handle the fact that a black man was covering sports in Milwaukee.

"Larry told me, "This is what happens to a talented black person. You're talented and some people find that threatening, but trust me. Understand that you might be threatening is actually a testament to your talent and ability, and it's your obligation to ignore these people and do what you what you do.'

"Larry showing me his hate mail inoculated me. "

Cal Thomas

"Any persecution I receive is nothing compared to what goes on in the rest of the world. Hate mail doesn't bother me. You won't be able to stop reading me."

Joanna Weiss

"When you're new to this, it's not your intention to generate email that can be so mean and personal. The Internet facilitates this. In the old days, you'd have to collect your thoughts, write a letter to the editor and there was a lot of space and time to express your gut reaction. Now there's no filter to putting out your reaction to the entire world. It really hurts civic discourse.

"I've gotten emails that hit me in the gut. It really bothers me when I think they didn't understand my point, and then I think it's a failure on my part. But if the email is nasty, then it doesn't merit a response, but the ones I ignore are rare. Early on in my TV reviewing career I tried to get into an exchange and match their tone. If someone got snarky, I'd get snarky, but it doesn't work. That's no way to get them to rethink their tone.

"Writing back is a way to put them on a different emotional plane. We can agree to disagree. Even if the person is angry, the follow up email has a much nicer tone after I've written back. Accept that many will disagree with your opinions."

Clarence Page

"Because I deal with controversy, I feel very disappointed if I don't get hate mail, it's like something went wrong. I did a couple of columns where apparently, I did too good of an argument, or I picked too soft of a target because I didn't get much mail at all.

"Normally, I get between 200-300 pieces of mail a day, and out of that maybe 10 to 20 percent pertains to what I've written. I want to mention the haters are my most loyal readers. I'm not the only columnist who says this. You can tell because they're the ones who will say, 'Oh, now you're saying so-and-so in your column, but on July 6, you said this.' So they're really paying attention.

"Once in a while I get attacked in the media, and once or twice I've gotten some really poignant, heartwarming notes from people who typically send me nothing but hate mail, calling me a commie, this and that, but one note said, "I saw somebody attacking you on TV for backing such and such, and I don't always agree with you, but I'd hate to see you go over something like that."

"Recently I was on vacation and coming back I was looking at my emails and this one fellow who is always sending me negative emails said, 'I haven't seen your column in a couple of weeks, I hope you're coming back.'

"I wrote back, 'Yes, thank you very much for asking. I'll be back in the paper tomorrow as ornery as ever.' I pay more attention to his name now when emails pop up. You get a relationship with people.

"I regret the brutalization of discourse that has occurred because of a lot of Internet features like opinion strings where you have people who write anonymously. They just rant and curse and they just want to show how big of an a-hole they can be, and I hate to reward them. At the *Tribune* right now, we have a system whereby you can't respond unless you register, it doesn't cost you anything to register as a *Tribune* reader, and that did a lot to reduce the anonymity and make the discourse more civil."

Stu Bykofsky

Stu Bykofsky is not an op-ed columnist. He is a long-time metro columnist with *The Philadelphia Daily News*, and his response is markedly different from the rest. In 2005 he spoke before the National Society of Newspaper Columnists in Grapevine, Texas, and his comments were deliciously pointed.

"The more poisonous, the better. If you think you can open up a can of whoop-ass on me, you're going to get back some sewage you're not going to want to see," Bykofsky told national columnists.

His best revenge is not giving those who write hateful emails the satisfaction of knowing their tirades were even read. Often he will send back this fake form reply:

Thank you very much, but unfortunately, Mr. Bykofsky doesn't have time to read email personally. Thank you. The Daily News Automated Response Team

Dave Lieber is now with the *Dallas Morning News*, after a long time career as a columnist for the *Fort Worth Star Telegram*. A national speaker, Lieber is the author of *The High-Impact Writer: Ideas, Tips & Strategies to Turn Your Writing World Upside Down*. The below excerpt from his book is reprinted with his gracious permission.

Forget About Being Popular

One of the hardest parts about The High-Impact Writer is that not everybody loves what you do. If you, like me, are the kind of person who wants people to like you (who doesn't?), then it will come as a shock that when you do high-impact writing, suddenly a whole bunch of people who you never knew don't like you.

I always say that if I were a reporter in a third-world nation who has done the kinds of reporting of stories that I did in the good ole U.S.A., I would have been killed a long time ago. I probably wouldn't have lasted very long in Louisiana either.

But America treats its truth-tellers a whole lot better than they do in Russia or Mexico. Only a few people have ever put a hand on me. The problem is those pesky letters to the editor and power brokers who feel they or their friends are the targets of your stories. They call your boss and try to get you removed from the story—or worse, get you fired.

But it's worth it—and unlike most of the people I write about who commit unethical acts, I'M STILL HERE!

There is little science about journalism, but there is one scientific theory that does work: For every reaction, there is going to be an opposite reaction.

What this means is that if you barge into somebody's office with your camera rolling to do The Great American Expose, well, when you leave, you can bet the farm that the head of that office will soon be on the phone with the head of your office.

What you did better follow policy and protocol in your workshop, or you are going to be in one heap o' trouble.

You must always tell your editor before you do something risky, so he/she can help you plan it out beforehand. And you always tell your editor immediately when something unexpected and potentially troubling has happened. That way, when the big shot calls your editor to complain about you, your editor already knows your side of the story. Remember that no manager likes to be surprised.

It's important that you have an editor on your side, supporting you. A good editor watches your back, and when the flack starts to come at you, a good editor will support you and defend your work. It doesn't always happen, but when it does, you've got to say a prayer of thanks to the gods of journalism.

One of the best-known editors in America, Dean Baquet, who ran *The Los Angeles Times* before he got fired for complaining about massive newsroom cutbacks, now works at *The New York Times*. Baquet once said:

"I think the newspaper should kick you around sometimes. I'd prefer you respect us more than love us...Our job is to ask tough questions of government. We should be tough, we should be believed, we should be vital. And that's a whole lot better than being loved."

I also love the quote from an old college newspaper colleague of mine. Noel Weyrich writes a monthly column for *Philadelphia* magazine in which he takes on the sacred cows of Philly's hierarchy. Noel once put it very succinctly when he wrote: "No one ever sees the light until they feel heat."

One of my mentors, mentioned earlier, is H.G. "Buzz" Bissinger, author of *Friday Night Lights* and a Pulitzer-prize winning reporter. A few years ago, Bissinger gave an interview *to Philadelphia Weekly* in which he criticized respected *Philadelphia Inquirer* columnist Tom Ferrick's nice-guy style.

Buzz' most memorable quote in that interview: "The purpose of a column isn't to hit a nice little shot down the middle of the fairway but to go for the green each and every time with passion and conviction and anger. Repeat after me, Tom: "It's OK to be a [jerk]. It's OK to be a [jerk]."

(Yes, I substituted a different word when I put in "jerk." Buzz used a different word.)

Even after I wrote columns for a decade, I still had a little problem dealing with critics. I felt like former First Lady Nancy Reagan, who once said that she would sit in the bathtub and have imaginary scolding matches with her husband's critics.

Developing a thick skin is tough. But I try to remember another quote supposedly uttered by *New York Times* columnist Thomas L. Friedman that you better have all your friends *before* you start writing a column because once you begin, you won't make any new ones.

Friends are overrated anyway

A few years ago, I had the single best year of my career. I was named Editorial Employee of the Year by the *Star-Telegram* and my annual job evaluation from my editors was glowing. But there was tradeoff. Some readers were aggravated by my aggressive writing and reporting style. They didn't want their columnist to be so, uh, high impact.

If readers wrote my annual review instead of my editors, it wouldn't have read the same. That same year as I was getting glowing commendations, I also went through my newspaper's Letter to the Editor section and collected readers' comments about my work.

I want to share a few:

Lieber is all about stirring up trouble. -J.G.

Having subscribed to the *Star-Telegram* for a year and having read Dave Lieber's tirades (unfounded, as far as I'm concerned), I cannot believe that he knows anything. -G.B.

I think Lieber goes overboard in his columns. -G.W.

Lieber has reinforced my contention that there is a liberal bias in the media. -P.C.

I'm disappointed in Lieber's values. -S.B.

Lieber is wrong. -R.H.

Whatever happened to unbiased, professional journalism? While reading Dave Lieber's column, I couldn't help wondering whether some personal vendetta or political agenda was at work. -J.B.

Having watched the brutal and cowardly stalking, sucker punch and tearful apology one National Hockey League player delivered to another, I couldn't help but notice the parallels with the writing style of columnist Dave Lieber. -A.F.

I feel sorry for Lieber and others who feel the need to cause trouble and stir dissension. Where's the good in that? -D.A.

I'm convinced that he has no clue about education, business and government issues and policies. -K.G.

I'm disgusted with Lieber's hypocrisy...Lieber should focus on the real issues, not chase rabbit trails. He should leave the hatchet at home. -M.D.

I used to have some modicum of respect for columnist Dave Lieber. I hereby call for Lieber's resignation/termination. -R.J.

As a "journalist" who promotes himself as a crusader against dishonesty and unethical conduct in government, Lieber should perhaps look in the mirror for an example of outrageous and unethical (not to mention insulting and offensive) conduct. Lieber owes an apology to the residents of our communities. To those who were confronted directly by him: I commend you for restraining yourselves from telling him what a jerk he is. He probably thought it was because you were afraid of what he might say in his column. -R.M.

So you may wonder how I deal with this. I'll admit that even as I retype these comments a few years later for you, they still sting a little. But then I remember what motivated each person to write what he/she did. In most cases, I was reporting straight facts with a little opinion (in my column) about wrongdoing or questionable behavior engaged in by public officials. Most of the folks who wrote the above comments for publication in the paper were sympathizers, family, friends or employees of the people I was writing about. There is little else to do to defend those you support than to either attack the story or attack the messenger.

When the story is inaccurate, critics attack the story. But when the story is accurate, they attack the messenger.

Notice they were never attacking my columns; it was always me. So how do I respond?

I guess I wear these comments with a badge of honor. And I know that many of the public officials whom I was writing about that led to the above comments, well, they are no longer in public life. And if you want to know why, you just have to read my stories.

Bottom line: The High-Impact Writer attracts plenty of critics. For every action, there is an opposite reaction. As long as The High-Impact Writer is accurate, fair and honest, he/she won't have much of a problem.

Two great minds in world history inspire me when I face such criticism:

We can easily forgive a child who is afraid of the dark. The real tragedy of life is when men are afraid of the light. -Plato

Never doubt that a small group of thoughtful, committed citizens can change the world; indeed, it is the only thing that ever does.
-Margaret Mead

BIOS OF FEATURED COLUMNISTS IN ALPHABETICAL ORDER

DAVE ASTOR is a journalist and reporter since 1983 and an award-winning op-ed humor columnist for *The Montclair* (N.J.) *Times* since 2003. (www.northjersey.com/news/opinions/montclairvoyant) He is a popular book blogger for *The Huffington Post*, a book reviewer who has been published in *The Washington Post*, the author of the 2012 memoir *Comic (and Column) Confessional: Finding Myself While Covering Syndicates, Celebrities, and a Changing Media World* (Xenos Press), and a board member of the National Society of Newspaper Columnists. Astor was formerly senior editor/syndication reporter for *Editor & Publisher* magazine, a newspaper reporter, and a magazine cartoonist.

JOEL BRINKLEY has worked in 46 states and more than 50 foreign countries for the last 30 years. His weekly op-ed column on foreign policy is syndicated with Tribune Media Services and he is featured on TMS' *American Voices*. Brinkley is the Hearst Professional in Residence for the journalism program at Stanford University, a position he assumed in 2006 after a 23-year career with *The New York Times*. There he served as a reporter and in the fall of 1979 he traveled to Cambodia to cover the fall of the Pol Pot regime and the resulting refugee crisis. For his stories, he won the Pulitzer Prize for International Reporting in 1980. Brinkley joined *The New York Times* Washington bureau in the fall of 1983, serving a wide variety of roles stateside and abroad, as well as serving as the White House and foreign policy correspondent, and the chief of the *Times* bureau in Jerusalem, Israel.

Brinkley is the author of several books: *The Circus Master's Mission*, a novel published by Random House in 1989; *Defining*

Vision: The Battle for the Future of Television, published by Harcourt Brace in 1998; *U.S. vs. Microsoft: The Inside Story of the Landmark Case* (with Steve Lohr) published by McGraw Hill in 2001; *Cambodia's Curse: The Modern History of a Troubled Land* published by Public Affairs Books in 2011.

Brinkley began his career with the Associated Press in Charlotte, N.C., in 1975 and then moved to the *Richmond (Va.) News Leader*, where he covered local and regional governments for three years. In 1977 he wrote a national series about the Ku Klux Klan and a new, little-known leader who seemed to be reviving it, named David Duke.

In 1978, he joined the staff of the *Louisville Courier-Journal*, where he served as a reporter, special projects writer and city editor. For the last 30 years, Brinkley has worked in 46 states and more than 50 foreign countries. He has won more than a dozen national reporting and writing awards, including a George Polk Award for national reporting. He served as a director for the Fund for Investigative Journalism for five years, until 2006.

Brinkley is a native of Washington, D.C., and a graduate of the University of North Carolina at Chapel Hill.

ELLEN GOODMAN has spent most of her life chronicling social change and its impact on American life. Ellen won the Pulitzer Prize for Distinguished Commentary in 1980. She's won many other awards, including the American Society of Newspaper Editors Distinguished Writing Award in 1980. She received the Hubert H. Humphrey Civil Rights Award from the Leadership Conference on Civil Rights in 1988. In 1993, The National Women's Political Caucus gave her the President's Award. In 1994, the Women's Research & Education Institute presented her with their American Woman Award. In 2008, she won the Ernie Pyle Award for Lifetime Achievement from the National Society of Newspaper columnists.

Ellen's first book, *Turning Points* (Doubleday, 1979), detailed the effects of the changing roles of women on the family. Six collections of her columns also have been published: *Close to Home* (Simon & Schuster, 1979); *At Large* (Summit Books, 1981); *Keeping in Touch* (Summit Books, 1985); *Making Sense* (Atlantic Monthly Press, 1989); and *Value Judgments* (Farrar Straus Giroux, 1993) and *Paper Trail: Common Sense in Uncommon Times* (Simon & Schuster, 2004). She is also co-author with Patricia O'Brien of *I Know Just What You Mean: The Power of Friendship in Women's Lives* (Simon & Schuster, 2000).

She began her career as a researcher for Newsweek magazine in the days when only men wrote for the newsweekly. She landed a job as a reporter for the *Detroit Free Press* in 1965 and, in 1967, for *The Boston Globe* where she began writing her column in 1974. Her column has been syndicated by the Washington Post Writers Group since 1976.

A 1963 cum laude graduate of Radcliffe College, Ellen returned to Harvard in 1973-74 as a Nieman Fellow, where she studied the dynamics of social change. In 2007, she was a Shorenstein Fellow at Harvard's Kennedy School of Government, where she studied gender and the news. As the first Lorry I. Lokey Visiting Professor in Professional Journalism she taught at Stanford in 1996.

Goodman retired in 2010, but continues as a writer, speaker and commentator. She co-found The Conversation Project in 2010 when a group of colleagues and concerned media, clergy, and medical professionals gathered to share stories of "good deaths" and "bad deaths" within their own circle of loved ones. Over several months, a vision emerged for a grassroots public campaign spanning both traditional and new media that would change our culture. The goal: to make it easier to initiate conversations about dying, and to encourage people to talk now and as often as necessary so that their wishes are known when the time comes.

Dr. MARK L. HOPKINS was president of four colleges during a 35-year career in higher education including Muscatine College (IA),

Elgin College (IL), Anderson University (SC) and Pacific States University (CA). In addition to his other responsibilities Dr. Hopkins was editor of two national newsletters, one for the Presidents of the nation's junior colleges (NCIJC) and the other for Presidents of all private college and university presidents (AAPICU). He was also appointed by Presidents Jimmy Carter, Ronald Reagan, and George H.W. Bush to serve on three national commissions for various higher education causes. He holds three degrees from Missouri universities.

Dr. Hopkins is a columnist for *The Anderson Independent-Mail* (SC) newspaper and the *Scripps* online newspapers as well as the GateHouse Media syndication group. He likes history and humor and both are reflected in his columns. Dr. Hopkins has published two books entitled *Facts and Opinions on the Issues of our Time, Books I and II*. Both are available through Amazon.com His column, Southern Perspective, can be found through the Independent Mail website (www.independentmail.com) and on GateHouse Media.

A well-traveled speaker, Dr. Hopkins has spoken at educational meetings in the U.S., Canada and Asia. His Asian speaking engagements include presentations in Korea, India, Sri Lanka and Viet Nam. For several years he served both the United Way of America and The National Speaker's Bureau as a regional and national speaker at conferences. His services were used by a variety of different national organizations including the American Association of Higher Education, The American Association of Community Colleges, The American Council on Education and the North Central Association.

Dr. Hopkins is a mid-westerner by birth and a southerner by choice. He lives in Anderson, South Carolina with his wife, Ruth. Together they have three grown children and six grand children.

DERRICK Z. JACKSON was a 2001 finalist for the Pulitzer Prize in commentary. A *Boston Globe* columnist since 1988, he is a two-time winner and three-time finalist for commentary awards from the National Education Writers Association and a five-time winner and twelve-time finalist for political and sports commentary from the National Association of Black Journalists.

He was the 2003 recipient of Columbia University's "Let's Do It Better," commentary awards and a 2004 winner for commentary from the National Lesbian and Gay Journalists Association. Jackson is also a three-time winner of the Sword of Hope commentary award from the New England Division of the American Cancer Society and a five-time winner of Unity journalism awards from Lincoln University in Missouri.

Prior to the Globe, Jackson won several awards at Newsday, including the 1985 Columbia University Meyer Berger Award for coverage of New York City and the 1979 award for feature writing from the Professional Basketball Writers Association. Jackson, born in 1955, is a native of Milwaukee, Wis., and is a 1976 graduate of the University of Wisconsin at Milwaukee. Jackson was a Nieman Fellow in Journalism at Harvard University in 1984. He holds honorary degrees from the Episcopal Divinity School in Cambridge, Mass., Salem State College in Salem, Mass., and the human rights award from Curry College in Milton, Mass.

ROBERT C. KOEHLER is a nationally recognized journalist, author and poet. Eschewing political labels, he considers himself a "peace journalist." He has been an editor at Tribune Media Services since 1995 and a TMS syndicated columnist since 1999. Over his 30-year career, Koehler has won national, state and local awards from the National Newspaper Association, Suburban Newspapers of America and several Peter Lisagor awards from the Chicago Headline Club.

His essays and columns have appeared in numerous newspapers and magazines and on public radio and the Internet. He is currently a regular contributor to such high-profile Web sites as the Huffington Post, Common Dreams, OpEd News and TruthOut; and is a sought-after speaker on such topics as election fraud and the nature of peace.

In his earlier career, he was a reporter, columnist and copy desk chief at Lerner Newspapers, a chain of neighborhood and suburban newspapers in the Chicago area. Koehler earned a master's degree in creative writing from Columbia College and taught writing at both the college and high school levels. Most satisfyingly, he developed innovative approaches to teaching writing to young people at several high schools on Chicago's West Side under the auspices of the Chicago Teachers Center.

Born in Detroit and raised in suburban Dearborn, Koehler slowly made his way west. After ten years in Kalamazoo, Mich., where he attended Western Michigan University, he moved to Chicago in 1976 where he still lives. Koehler is a widower and single parent. He explores both conditions at great depth in his writing.

DAVE LIEBER is the new consumer columnist for *The Dallas Morning News*. Known largely for his twice-weekly "Watchdog" column in the *Fort Worth Star-Telegram* for the past 20 years, he will bring his brand of investigative energy and what he has dubbed "Watchdog Nation common sense" to a twice-a-week column, appearing Fridays and Sundays.

Aside from creating his WatchdogNation.com consumer rights movement, Dave also created his all-volunteer charity, Summer Santa, which provides assistance for impoverished children in North Texas.

"Dave has one of the most trusted voices in North Texas and our newsroom is honored to have him here," said Bob Mong, editor of *The Dallas Morning News*. "For 20 years, people in Tarrant County knew they had an advocate, someone in their corner to help them solve problems with business or government. We're lucky to have him, and we think readers across the region will feel likewise."

Lieber won the Will Rogers Humanitarian Award in 2002 from the National Society of Newspaper Columnists, for work that "best exemplifies the high ideals of the beloved philosopher-humorist who used his platform for the benefit of his fellow human beings." Lieber is also a sought-after speaker, appearing in front of more than 100 audiences each year. He is the author of *The High Impact Writer: Ideas, Tips and Strategies to Turn Your Writing World Upside Down* that features skills and techniques from his longtime career. His website is www.yankeecowboy.com

MICHAEL R. MASTERSON is a journalist, editor and columnist. Since 2000 to present his op-ed column runs three times a week in the *Arkansas Democrat Gazette*. His 40+ year career includes investigative reporting for *The Ashbury Park Press, The Arizona Republic* (investigative team leader), *WEHCO Media* (six daily papers in Arkansas), *The Chicago Sun Times* (investigative team leader) and *The Los Angeles Times* (staff reporter). He worked as an editor for *The Northwest Arkansas Times, The Hot Springs Sentinel* and *The Newport Daily Independent*.

His awards include the 2012 The Will Rogers Humanitarian Award from National Society of Newspaper Columnists, two National Headliner Awards for writing and reporting; four-time award-winner in Robert F. Kennedy Awards; three-time award-winner in Heywood Broun Memorial Awards; Twice finalist for Pulitzer Prize (national and specialized reporting), George Polk Award for national reporting; four-time winner of Paul Tobenkin Memorial Award from Graduate School of Journalism at Columbia University for fighting against bigotry and hatred; twice winner of the Investigative Reporters and Editors (IRE) newspaper award, including Gold Medallion representing "best of the best;" Arkansas Journalist of the Year 1986; National Assn. of Black Journalists first place prize for reporting on the "black condition;" National Congress of American Indians Congressional Award for investigative reporting that exposed massive corruption in federal Indian programs; Mass Media Gold Medallion from National Conference of Christians and Jews for promoting "brotherhood and understanding;" Best of the West investigative project reporting; twice winner in Champion Media Awards for advancement of economic understanding from Dartmouth University. Twice winner of the Clarion Award from

U.S. Women in Communications for best large newspaper column writing and investigative reporting; Three citations from American Bar Association for investigative stories within the legal system. Many state awards for investigative reporting, editorial writing and feature writing. Reporting also has prompted reforms in various state systems, including the Arkansas State Crime Laboratory. Now an independent contributor, Masterson works from his homes in Fayetteville and Santa Fe.

CLARENCE PAGE, the 1989 Pulitzer Prize winner for Commentary, has been a columnist and a member of the *Chicago Tribune's* editorial board since July 1984. His column is syndicated nationally by Tribune Media Services. He also participated in a *Chicago Tribune* vote fraud investigation, which won the 1972 Pulitzer Prize for public service. He shared a 1980 Illinois UPI award for an investigative series titled "The Black Tax" and a 1976 Edward Scott Beck Award for overseas reporting in Southern Africa. In 1992, he was inducted into the Chicago Journalism Hall of Fame and later received a lifetime achievement award from the National Association of Black Journalists. His 1996 book, *Showing My Color: Impolite Essays on Race and Identity*, was published by HarperCollins. From 1980 to 1984 Page also worked at WBBM-TV in Chicago as a news reporter, a talk show host and director of community affairs. He received his Bachelor of Science in journalism degree from Ohio University in 1969. Born in Dayton, Ohio, began his journalism career as a freelance writer and photographer for the Middletown Journal and Cincinnati Enquirer at the age of 17. He and his wife Lisa have one son and reside in the Washington DC area.

KATHLEEN PARKER started her column in 1987 when she was a staff writer for *The Orlando Sentinel*. Her column was nationally syndicated in 1995 and she joined The Washington Post Writers Group in 2006. She is also a contributor to the online magazine, *The Daily Beast*, and is a consulting faculty member at the Buckley School of Public Speaking. She served on USA Today's Board of

Contributors and wrote for its op-ed page. Parker won the Pulitzer Prize for Commentary in 2010 for her political op-ed column. *The Week* magazine named her one of the nation's Top Five columnists in 2004 and 2005.In 1993 the *Baltimore Sun* presented her with the H. L. Mencken writing award. Parker is the author of *Save the Males: Why Men Matter, Why Women Should Care* (New York: Random House, 2008). Parker is a regular guest on NBC's *The Chris Matthews Show*. In 2010 Parker and Eliot Spitzer, former governor of New York, co-hosted *Parker Spitzer*, a cable news program for CNN.

CONNIE SCHULTZ is a journalist, syndicated columnist and author. Her op-ed columns been syndicated with Creators Syndicate since 2007, and her column, *Views*, has been published by *Parade Magazine* since 2010. She was a reporter and columnist for the *Cleveland Plain Dealer* newspaper from 1993 to 2011. Schultz won the 2005 Pulitzer Prize for Distinguished Commentary, and was a finalist for the 2003 Pulitzer Prize in feature writing. Schultz is the recipient of the Robert F. Kennedy Award for Social Justice Reporting, the National Headliner Award's Best of Show and journalism awards from both Harvard College and Columbia University. In 2004, Schultz won the Batten Medal, which honors "a body of journalistic work that reflects compassion, courage, humanity and a deep concern for the underdog."

She is the author of *Life Happens: And Other Unavoidable Truths* (Random House 2006) and the book, *And His Lovely Wife: A Memoir From the Woman Beside the Man*, (Random House 2007) about her experiences on the campaign trail with her husband, U.S. Senator Sherrod Brown (D-Ohio).

JEFFREY L. SEGLIN is a journalist, author and teacher. His column, *The Right Thing*, runs in newspapers throughout the U.S. and in Canada. In it he offers solutions to ethical dilemmas posed by readers. From 2004 to 2010 the New York Times Syndicate carried *The Right Thing*. Then Tribune Media Service distributed his column from 2010 to present. Seglin is the Director of the Communications Program at the John F. Kennedy School of Government at Harvard where he is a lecturer in public policy and teaches opinion writing.

He is the author of *The Right Thing: Conscience, Profit and Personal Responsibility in Today's Business*, which was named a Best Business Book for 2003 by the *Library Journal*. He also wrote, *The Good, the Bad, and Your Business: Choosing Right When Ethical Dilemmas Pull You Apart* (Wiley, 2000). He is the author or co-author on more than a dozen books on business and writing, and has written for various publications, such as *The New York Times, Real Simple, Fortune, FSB, Salon.com, Time.com, Sojourners, MIT's Sloan Management Review, Harvard Management Update, Business 2.0, Forbes ASAP*, and has contributed commentaries to Public Radio's Marktplace.

From 1999 until 2011 at Emerson College in Boston, Seglin was an associate professor and director of the graduate program in publishing and writing. He has been an ethics fellow at the Poynter Institute for Media Studies since 2001 and was a resident fellow at the Center for the Study of Values in Public Life at Harvard University in 1998-1999.

He was the host of *Doing Well by Doing Good*, an hour-long live television program for WCVE-TV, PBS's Richmond Virginia affiliate. Nationally, Seglin lectures widely on ethics, business ethics, and writing, and is represented by American Talent Group for speaking engagements.

CAL THOMAS is syndicated with Tribune Media Service, which deems him the number one syndicated political columnist, with a twice-weekly column appearing in more than 500 newspapers nationwide. A graduate of American University, Thomas is a 40-year veteran of broadcast and print journalism. He has worked for NBC, CNBC, and PBS television. In 1997 he joined Fox News Channel as a political contributor and appears weekly on the media critique show, *Fox News Watch*. He has appeared on *NBC Nightly*

News, Nightline, The Today Show, Good Morning America, CNN Crossfire, Larry King Live, and the *Oprah Winfrey Show*. His *USA TODAY* feature, "Common Ground," discusses contentious social issues with his friend and political counterpart, Bob Beckel. In 1995, Thomas hosted his own program on CBNC and was honored with a Cable Ace Award nomination for Best Interview Program. Other awards include a George Foster Peabody team reporting award, and awards from both the Associated Press and United Press International.

Thomas has authored 11 books, *Common Ground: How to Stop the Partisan War That is Destroying America* (co-authored with Bob Beckel), *Blinded by Might: Can the Religious Right Save America?, Things That Matter Most, The Wit and Wisdom of Cal Thomas, Book Burning, Liberals for Lunch, Occupied Territory, Public Persons and Private Lives, The Death of Ethics in America, A Freedom Dream* and *Uncommon Sense*. Thomas is a national speaker, lecturing frequently at college campuses and appearing before nonprofit and corporate audiences. He lives with his wife, Ray, in the Washington, D. C. area. They have four children and eight grandchildren.

LYNNE VARNER is a journalist, columnist, author and public speaker. Her column for The Seattle Times runs every other Friday and Varner blogs daily for Northwest Opinion and muses nonstop on Twitter at @lkvarner.

As a member of the Editorial Board, Varner charts the paper's institutional voice on education, social issues and race and class. Varner was nominated for a Pulitzer Prize in 2006 for a series of columns about the U.S. Supreme Court's review of the use of racial preferences in Seattle's public schools. Varner also received a John S. Knight Fellowship and spent an academic year studying race and politics at Stanford University.

She grew up outside of Washington, D.C. and is a graduate of the University of Maryland, College Park. She worked for United Press

International and The Washington Post before moving to Seattle to work for the Seattle Post-Intelligencer. She lives with her husband and young son outside of Seattle.

Among her other outside interests, Varner is a quilter and fiber artist. She is the co-author of *Stories That Cover Us: Meditations and Fiber Art by Pacific Northwest African American Quilters*. http://www.blurb.com/b/698430-stories-that-cover-us

JOANNA WEISS writes an op-ed column about culture, politics and society for *The Boston Globe*. Her columns appear, via the *New York Times* newswire, in newspapers across the country. She frequently appears on local and national television and radio. She has also written for *The Economist* and *Slate*. Previously, Weiss was a political reporter, feature writer, and television critic for the *Globe*. She started her career covering Louisiana politics at the *Times-Picayune* of New Orleans. She is the author of the novel *Milkshake*, a comic send-up of motherhood and feminism. Weiss lives in Milton, Massachusetts with her husband, son and daughter.

Acknowledgments

The Creator allowed me to share the hard-won advice from the extraordinary and talented columnists in this book. Thank you for giving me both potential and a purpose.

My husband David Standring, daughter Starleen, son-in-law Joseph Baylon and granddaughters Bella and Lulu are the love, light and laughter in my life. Without you, nothing would be written.

During this adventure, each featured columnist was gracious, supportive and patient, especially with my many "one more thing" emails. Thank you for your candor and vulnerability.

Richard Connolly applied his keen eye, editing talent and insight to my manuscript. Thank you for a treasured friendship and the gift of time.

I am indebted to my colleagues at the National Society of Newspaper Columnists where it all began.

Taking center stage for a bow are my dear friend and colleague Don McNay and RRP International's Adam Turner who lifted me into RRP's galaxy. Truly, you treat all your authors like supernovas and it's my blessing to be hitched to your star.

I hug my family and dear friends. Thank you for seeing me through my stumbling and grumbling on the long road of drafts and rewrites. Finis is a beautiful word!

About the Author

Suzette Martinez Standring

SUZETTE MARTINEZ STANDRING is syndicated with GateHouse Media for her spirituality column and blog, *Spiritual Café*. She took first place for Online, Blog and Multimedia columns (for circulation under 100,000) in the 2013 competition for the National Society of Newspaper Columnists. She hosts and produces *It's All Write With Suzette,* a writing show that features guest authors and columnists on Milton (MA) Cable TV Access. She is the award-winning author of *The Art of Column Writing: Insider Secrets from Art Buchwald, Dave Barry, Arianna Huffington, Pete Hamill and Other Great Columnists.* She is a past president of The National Society of Newspaper Columnists, and teaches writing workshops nationally. A San Francisco native, she now calls Massachusetts home. She is happily married, the mother of one daughter and blessed with two grandchildren. When writing block happens, she takes her little dog for a walk and lead paragraphs fall out of the trees.

Her newest book is *The Art of Opinion Writing: Insider Secrets from Top Op-Ed Columnists.*

Praise for The Art of Opinion Writing

"Op-ed writing goes beyond newspaper essays. Anyone who can make a written argument worthy of an op-ed column is a writer who knows how to influence others to make the world a better place. And that's exactly what most writers want to do anyway."
Dave Lieber, *Dallas Morning News*

"Martinez Standring masterfully delves deep into the thought processes of some of the nation's best-known op-ed writers. This insightful, inside look at how they frame their writing is a must-read for anyone interested in learning how to craft high-quality opinion and commentary pieces."
Eric Heyl, 2013 President, National Society of Newspaper Columnists

"Suzette's wonderful book explores the highly individual art of opinion writing, honoring the craft by giving its practitioners a chance to reveal their secrets. This is fascinating reading for anyone interested in plumbing the mysteries of journalism."
Robert Koehler, Tribune Media Service

"Suzette has a unique gift. She can make a complicated topic simple and a mundane topic interesting. She gives people the opportunity to learn by studying the best and communicates in a way that make you want to grab the book and see what is on the next page."
Don McNay, best-selling author and syndicated columnist.

"It's quite a trick to educate, entertain and/or persuade in roughly 700 words, and Suzette Standring reveals the secrets of some of the best. Each perspective is a little different, I can't agree with all of them, but it's fun to see what makes them tick."
Stu Bykofsky, Columnist, *Philadelphia Daily News*

"Suzette Martinez Standring, author of the engaging and educational The Art of Column Writing, *has done it again with this superb book about op-ed writing. In it, she discusses the importance of the op-ed craft, what makes a great op-ed writer, the variety of op-ed approaches, and much more. Even more compelling are the thoughts of renowned op-ed columnists. Stellar writing, extensive knowledge, and warm humanity are in full evidence in this book."* Dave Astor, op-ed columnist for *The Montclair* (N.J.) *Times,* The Huffington Post blogger, vice president of the National Society of Newspaper Columnists and author of *Comic (and Column) Confessional.*

Check out these other great titles!

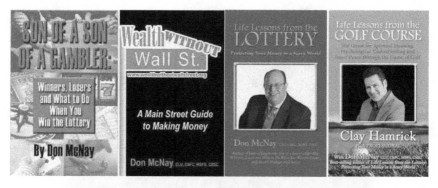

CPSIA information can be obtained
at www.ICGtesting.com
Printed in the USA
LVHW051500300120
645335LV00002B/275